C000262232

FABER PLAYWRIGHTS
AT THE NATIONAL THEATRE

Faber Playwrights
at the National Theatre

faber and faber

First published in 2005
by Faber and Faber Limited
3 Queen Square, London WC1N 3AU

Typeset by Country Setting, Kingsdown, Kent CT14 8ES
Printed in England by Mackays of Chatham plc, Chatham, Kent

Alan Bennett, David Hare, Tom Stoppard, Tony Harrison,
Christopher Hampton and Frank McGuinness are hereby
identified as authors of this work in accordance with
Section 77 of the Copyright, Designs and Patents Act 1988

A CIP record for this book
is available from the British Library

ISBN 0-571-23076-8

2 4 6 8 10 9 7 5 3 1

Contents

Introduction

This series of conversations with Faber playwrights was one of the events marking Faber's seventy-fifth anniversary and took place at the National Theatre in 2004.

When I was first published by Faber they were still in their Woburn Place premises overlooking Russell Square. T. S. Eliot was not long dead and some of his austerity still hung about the building, which I had ventured into several times to call on Mary-Kay Wilmers, who worked there for a while before departing for *The Listener* and, later, the *London Review of Books*. Through Mary-Kay I got to know Charles Monteith and Rosemary Goad, and so when *Forty Years On* was staged in 1968 I took it to Faber as they were the only publishers I knew.

At that time they were known more as publishers of poetry, with plays still something of a sideline. Frank Pike was my first editor and I am glad to find him recalled by several of the playwrights in this book as he was always a reassuring presence, particularly if a play hadn't gone well. There was the occasional tiff. I took it badly when Faber ceased to publish plays in hardback. Or ceased to publish my plays in hardback: they still, I noted at the time, published Tom Stoppard in hardback. With no satisfactory explanation forthcoming, I thought of decamping (sic) to Methuen or Nick Hern, but probably forgot. Nowadays I couldn't imagine going anywhere else, Peggy Paterson and her successor Dinah Wood having been so energetic on my behalf (and on behalf of the drama generally, of course).

Still, I've never felt part of a stable, and playwriting being a pretty solitary business there's no reason why one should ever meet one's fellow practitioners. Which is another reason to welcome this book. Still, I am relieved not to have been asked to take part, as my colleagues seem enviably articulate and, unlike me when in front of an audience, capable of long stretches of coherent thought. Or maybe that's the editing – by Lyn Haill at the National.

Their audiences, too, seem more serious-minded than the ones I often attract, and commendably well-informed about the playwrights' work and with a perspective on it, too, which is more than critics often manage. Welcome are the sidelights on the practical business of putting a play together, though I'd have liked a bit more of their disasters and some reassurance about all the hanging about that playwriting seems to involve, for me anyway. It's good finally to read Tony Harrison's tribute to the much-missed Jocelyn Herbert. There can have been few more fruitful collaborations between playwright and designer than theirs or any that ended so poignantly.

This collection of interviews is only on sale in the NT Bookshop. It's a friendly and lively institution for which playwrights, not merely at the National, must be grateful as they sell a lot of copies both of plays and books on drama generally. In the intervals of the performance the bookshop is often as crowded as the bar. Long may it continue.

Alan Bennett
September 2005

David Hare

5 NOVEMBER 2004
LYTTELTON THEATRE

Cast performing the extract:

M. Aung Chooi Beh
Sir Leonard Darwin Bill Nighy
Raymond Brock Julian Rhind-Tutt
Susan Traherne Nancy Carroll
Mme. Aung Sara Houghton
Alice Parkes Eleanor Howell

DAVID HARE This is the first in a series of 'Platforms' to mark the seventy-fifth anniversary of the publishing house of Faber and Faber, which publishes a great many playwrights and has published my plays for nearly thirty-five years.

When I first wrote a play, in 1970, it was quite unusual for plays to be published. There were two principal publishing houses for drama: Methuen, which then had Harold Pinter and other modern playwrights, and Faber, which asked me for my first play. Because it was the publishing house of John Osborne and Samuel Beckett, it wasn't very difficult to agree. In publishing plays, Faber has always given them the status of literature. After all, when I joined, this was the publishing house of T. S. Eliot, of W. H. Auden, of Sylvia Plath and of Ted Hughes, in fact some of the best poetry of the day. Faber, unlike most publishing houses, sees the performing arts as literature. In this country – unlike in France – there's a terrible division between the book pages and the performing arts pages in newspapers. When you talk about literature, it isn't usually taken by the literary world to include plays, films and television. But to me, and to all the people I respect, a large portion of what's interesting in British literature has happened in my adult life in the performing arts rather than on the printed page. What is wonderful about Faber is that the house has given play publication literary status. Nowadays, I don't see how a publisher can call itself a serious literary house if it doesn't publish plays. Recently, Faber has published film scripts as well, lured by Quentin Tarantino into believing that people wanted to read filmscripts.

Perhaps the lesson they have learnt is that people do want to read Tarantino scripts, but not scripts by the rest of us.

Faber has asked a group of playwrights to choose the play that was most significant in our publishing history, so that's why we're going to do a bit of *Plenty* tonight.

The history of *Plenty* is this. I worked first at the National Theatre for Laurence Olivier in 1971. When Peter Hall became Artistic Director, he asked me to work for him originally as a director. In fact, in 1976, I directed the first play to originate in this building, in this very theatre, the Lyttelton – a terrific play of Howard Brenton's called *Weapons of Happiness*. Then Peter asked me if I would also write a play for the National. I said I wanted to write about the Second World War, and I could see his face fall. It's hard to think back to the 1970s, when the idea that we had of the Second World War came almost entirely from Kenneth More and Richard Todd, and all those patriotic movies like *Reach for the Sky*, which represented the war as a sort of jaunt, essentially about courage, and, if you like, Manichean: the good fought the bad, the good were good throughout, the bad were bad throughout, and we won. I could see Peter thinking, 'Oh my God, he's going to write about the Second World War. I don't look forward to this.'

In fact, I went off and conceived a television play for the BBC, *Licking Hitler*, which I wrote alongside *Plenty* – I wrote the two plays together. They were an attempt to begin a radical reinterpretation of what had happened during the war, and were very much inspired by a book of Angus Calder's, *The People's War*. Angus Calder is a social historian who looked at the war not from the viewpoint of the officer class but of the soldiers. He argues that the sacking of Churchill after the war was not in fact an anomaly, as it's usually represented in British history – Churchill won the war and then the British threw him out. On the contrary, what had happened was that people had gone to war and been radicalised by it. For the first time in their lives they were meeting the officer class, often judging them to be incompetent, and through their direct experience of the officer class, coming back and wanting a world which was much much better.

Licking Hitler is centred on the war and then briefly, at the end, deals with the peace. *Plenty* deals very briefly with the war and then largely is concerned with the peace. They are both about women, because women served an extraordinary function in the war, often were involved in some of the greatest acts of bravery, and were completely overlooked by the official accounts. *Licking Hitler* concerns a woman who works in Black Propaganda during the war, and *Plenty* concerns a woman who has been flown behind the lines for the SOE [Special Operations Executive] into France. I was very struck by a statistic I found in a history book which was that 75 per cent of the women who served in the SOE divorced in the years following the war. It became clear to me, meeting these women, that they had found it very hard to construct lives afterwards. The contrast between the war and the peace was almost unbearable to them; they had seen so many extraordinary acts of courage, so many people behaving at their very, very best, that they just didn't know how to make a daily life, having lived at that extraordinary pitch for those years. My heroine in *Plenty*, Susan Traherne, is somebody who can't adapt to post-war life.

The play was done in the Lyttelton in 1978. It had the most wonderful cast and was very brilliantly performed, particularly on the first night – which was a complete disaster. In my memory, the main problem was the sheer unpleasantness of the audience – they were just a *horrible* audience. Sure enough, we were not well reviewed. We were antagonistically reviewed, particularly by Bernard Levin on the *Sunday Times*, who was a man who always was 'on my case', as they say, and determined that nothing I could do could be any good. He even said that this was the play with the most obscure title since *Twelfth Night*. Well, for a start the title of *Twelfth Night* is perfectly clear, everybody knows it is called *Twelfth Night* because it was performed on Twelfth Night – clear as day! Similarly, the title of *Plenty* is clear as day – it's a play about the difference between the austerity of war and the flush of affluence that arrived in the fifties. That's why it's called *Plenty*. Levin basically tore the play to shreds.

We had what they call a 'nervous' situation in the Lyttelton, where we were playing to roughly 40 per cent. The board of the theatre asked Peter Hall to take the play off. Peter Hall said, 'What is the point of subsidised theatre if we can't do work we believe in? I believe I can protect this play.' This is one of the advantages of repertory. He played it twice a week, often on Fridays and Saturdays, which are good theatregoing nights, so that it could build an audience. That's the reason I wanted particularly to talk about *Plenty* tonight; because I owe so much to Peter's loyalty and belief in the play. It was a crucial turning point in my life as a playwright that Peter insisted, against his Board's wishes, on letting the play run. As it ran, both Kate Nelligan's performance in the central role and the play itself began to acquire a public by word of mouth. After a nine-month run, it was then full for the last three months. It was the deeply, deeply satisfying thing of beating the critics, which can only happen in the subsidised theatre; it can't happen in commercial theatre, and, as Peter asserted, it's what a national theatre is for. Yes, of course you must take off work that you're not pleased with and don't believe in. But if you do something that you know is good and yet is not recognised as good, this organisation exists to go on asserting that it's good and not merely to judge it by commercial criteria. It's the first lesson of subsidised theatre – the job is to lead public taste not to follow it.

Then Joseph Papp, after four years of prevaricating, agreed to produce it in New York, and he did that, he told me very bad-temperedly, only to stop people telling him to produce it. Joe Papp was a hero of the American theatre in all sorts of ways, not least because he wanted a Hispanic and African-American theatre. He said the laziest way to run a theatre in America is to do British hits. From the very start, although he had done my first play *Slag*, he said he was not going to import plays from Britain because it was vital to get a broad ethnic mix into his theatre. That was the reason he became the most important producer in America. He brought black writers and actors to the Public Theatre way before anyone else started considering that that was an important thing to do. But he gave in on *Plenty*, because he said it was the kind of play he wished he could get Americans to write. And there it met with an approval which it has never met with in this country.

It was the first time in my life that I'd ever experienced wholehearted approval. It's a very extraordinary experience, for a playwright, it isn't like anything else. You don't get it in England – or at least I never have – but you do get it abroad. It was heaven. I remember Kate Nelligan saying to me, 'Even you can't pick a hole in this.' The Americans were not upset by the portrait of Britain in the play. They felt less implicated, if you like, in the way that it represents Englishness. They saw it much more as a play about Vietnam, they saw the parallel with their own attitudes to what had happened in Vietnam. They didn't feel criticised, whereas the people who disliked *Plenty*, of whom there were many, felt that it was critical of them. When it was revived five years ago, with Cate Blanchett, in a production by Jonathan Kent for the Almeida, then it was very satisfying to see that it had lost none of its power to offend and upset. It was startling how the passages in the play that had caused most offence in 1978 were still causing a great deal of offence in the nineties – in particular a scene in which Susan Traherne essentially uses a man to get herself pregnant. This still upsets the theatregoing public, or rather one section of the theatregoing public. It was quite extraordinary to sit in the theatre and feel men still being offended by a woman's right to treat a man as a sperm-donor. And the shock of the underlying critique in *Plenty* still sent a lot of people very angry out of the theatre.

So that's the history of the play; and here's the extract.

Knightsbridge. October 1956.
From the dark, music, emphatic, triumphant.
The room we saw in Scene One [then stripped of furniture]. But now decorated with heavy velvet curtains, china objects and soft furniture. A diplomatic home. Both men in dinner-jackets: Brock smokes a cigar and drinks brandy. Opposite him is an almost permanently smiling Burmese, M. Aung, short, dogmatic. The music stops.

Aung Two great nations, sir. The Americans and the English. Like the Romans and the Greeks. Americans are the Romans – power, armies, strength. The English are the Greeks – ideas, civilisation, intellect. Between them they shall rule the world.

Darwin appears, putting his head round the door. He is also in a dinner-jacket. He appears exhausted.

Darwin Good Lord, I hope you haven't hung on for me.

Brock Leonard, come in, how kind of you to come.

Darwin Not at all.

Brock ushers him in. Aung stands.

Brock Our little gathering. We'd scarcely dared hope . . .

Darwin There seemed nothing left to do.

Brock Leonard, you know Monsieur Aung, of course?

8

Aung Mr Darwin.

Darwin Rangoon.

Brock Now First Secretary, Burmese Embassy.

Aung An honour. A privilege. A moment in my career. I shake your hand. (*He does so.*)

Darwin Good, good. Well . . .

Brock Let me get you a drink.

Darwin That would be very kind.

Brock I'll just tell my wife you're here.

Brock goes out. Aung smiles at Darwin.

Aung Affairs of state?

Darwin Yes, if you . . .

Aung Say no more. We have eaten. We did not wait. In Burma we say if you cannot be on time, do not come at all.

Darwin Really?

Aung But of course the English it is different. At your command the lion makes its bed with the lamb.

Darwin Hardly.

Aung Don't worry. All will be well. Ah, Darwin of Djakarta, to have met the man, to have been alone with him. I shall dine in on this for many years.

Darwin Dine out on this.

Aung Ah, the English language, she is a demanding mistress, yes?

Darwin If you like.

Aung And no one controls her so well as you, sir. You beat her and the bitch obeys. (*He laughs.*) The language of the world. Good, good. I have learnt the phrase from you. Out of your mouth. Good, good. I am behind you, sir.

Susan appears in a superbly cut evening dress. She is dangerously cheerful. Brock follows her.

Susan Leonard, how good of you to make an appearance.

Darwin I'm only sorry I've been delayed.

Susan and Darwin kiss.

Susan Brock says you're all ragged with fatigue. I hear you've been having the most frightful week . . .

Darwin It has been, yes.

Susan Well, don't worry. Here at least you can relax. You've met Monsieur Aung?

Darwin Indeed.

Susan You can forget everything. The words 'Suez Canal' will not be spoken.

Darwin That will be an enormous relief.

Susan They are banned, you will not hear them.

Darwin Thank you, my dear.

Susan Nasser, nobody will mention his name.

Darwin Quite.

Susan Nobody will say 'blunder' or 'folly' or 'fiasco'. Nobody will say 'international laughing stock'. You are among friends, Leonard. I will rustle up some food.

She smiles at Aung.

Mr Aung, I think the gentlemen may wish to talk.

Aung Of course, in such company I am privileged to change sex.

Aung gets up to follow Susan out.

Susan Nobody will say 'death-rattle of the ruling class'. We have stuck our lips together with marron glacé. I hope you understand.

Susan and Aung go out. Pause.

Brock Sorry, I . . .

Darwin It's all right.

Brock I did ask her to calm down.

Darwin I'm getting used to it.

Brock She's been giving me hell. She knows how closely you've been involved . . .

Darwin Do you think we could leave the subject, Brock?

Pause.

I'm eager for the drink.

Brock Of course.

Darwin At least she got rid of that appalling wog. I mean, in honesty, Raymond, what are you trying to do to me?

Brock I'm sorry, sir.

Darwin This week of all weeks. He had his tongue stuck so far up my fundament all you could see of him were the soles of his feet.

Brock takes over a tray of drinks.

Mental illness, is it? Your wife?

Brock No, she just . . . feels very strongly. Well, you know . . .

Darwin But there has been mental illness?

Brock In the past.

Darwin Yes?

Brock Before we were married. Some years ago. She'd been living very foolishly, a loose set in Pimlico. And a series of jobs, pushing herself too hard. Not eating. We got engaged when she was still quite ill, and I have tried to help her back up.

Darwin That's very good.

Brock Well . . .

Darwin Second marriage, of course. Often stabilises.

Brock What?

Darwin The chap in Brussels.

Pause.

The stiff.

Brock Ah yes.

Darwin You don't have to be ashamed . . .

Brock No, I'm not, it's . . .

Darwin In the diplomatic service it isn't as if a mad wife is any kind of professional disadvantage. On the contrary, it almost guarantees promotion.

Brock Well . . .

Darwin Some of the senior men, their wives are absolutely barking. I take the word 'gouache' to be the giveaway. When they start drifting out of rooms saying, 'I think I'll just go and do my gouaches, dear,' then you know you've lost them for good and all.

Brock But Susan isn't mad.

Darwin No, no.

Pause.

Is there a Madame Aung?

Brock In the other room.

Darwin I knew there had to be. Somehow. And no doubt culturally inclined. Traditional dance, she'll tell us about, in the highlands of Burma. Or the plot of *Lohengrin*.

Brock Leonard . . .

Darwin I'm sorry. I think I've had it, Brock. One more Aung and I throw in the can.

Pause.

Do you mind if I have a cherry?

Brock What?

Darwin The maraschinos. I'm so hungry. It's all those bloody drugs we have to take.

Brock Let me . . .

Darwin Stay.

Pause.

We have been betrayed.

Darwin reaches into the cocktail cherries with his fingers, but then just rolls them slowly in his palm.

We claim to be intervening as a neutral party in a dispute between Israel and Egypt. Last Monday the Israelis launched their attack. On Tuesday we issued our ultimatum saying both sides must withdraw to either side of the canal. But, Raymond, the Israelis, the aggressors, they were nowhere near the canal. They'd have had to advance a hundred miles to make the retreat.

Brock Who told you that?

Darwin Last week the Foreign Secretary went abroad. I was not briefed. We believe he met with the French and the Israelis, urged the Israelis to attack. I believe our ultimatum was written in France last week, hence the mistake in the wording. The Israelis had reckoned to reach the canal, but met with unexpectedly heavy resistance. I think the entire war is a fraud cooked up by the British as an excuse for seizing the canal. And we, we who have to execute this policy, even we were not told.

Pause.

Brock Well . . . what difference does it make?

Darwin My dear boy.

Brock I mean it.

Darwin Raymond.

Brock It makes no difference.

Darwin I was lied to.

Brock Yes, but you were against it from the start.

Darwin I . . .

Brock Oh come on, we all were. The Foreign Office hated the operation from the very first mention, so what difference does it make now?

Darwin All the difference in the world.

Brock None at all.

Darwin The government lied to me.

Brock If the policy was wrong, if it was wrong to begin with . . .

Darwin They are not in good faith.

Brock I see, I see, so what you're saying is, the British may do anything, doesn't matter how murderous, doesn't matter how silly, just so long as we do it in good faith?

Darwin Yes. I would have defended it, I wouldn't have minded how damn stupid it was. I would have defended it had it been honestly done. But this time we are cowboys and when the English are the cowboys, then in truth I fear for the future of the globe.

A pause. Darwin walks to the curtained window and stares out. Brock, left sitting, doesn't turn as he speaks.

Brock Eden is weak. For years he has been weak. For years people have taunted him, why aren't you strong? Like Churchill? He goes round, he begins to think I must find somebody to be strong on. He finds Nasser. Now he'll show them. He does it to impress. He does it badly. No one is impressed.

Darwin turns to look at Brock.

Mostly what we do is what we think people expect of us. Mostly it's wrong.

Pause.

Are you going to resign?

The sound of laughter as Susan, Mme Aung, M. Aung and Alice stream into the room. Mme Aung is small, tidy and bright. Alice is spectacularly dressed.

Susan Madame Aung has been enthralling us with the story of the new Bergman film at the Everyman.

Darwin Ah.

Brock Ah yes.

Susan Apparently it's about depression, isn't that so, Madame Aung?

Mme Aung I do feel the Norwegians are very good at that sort of thing.

Susan Is anything wrong?

Susan stands and looks at Brock and Darwin.

Please do sit down, everyone. I'm sorry, I think we may have interrupted the men.

Brock It's all right.

Susan They were probably drafting a telegram . . .

Brock We weren't . . .

Susan That's what they do before they drop a bomb. They send their targets notice in a telegram. Bombs tonight, evacuate the area. Now what does that indicate to you, Monsieur Aung?

Brock Susan, please.

Susan I'll tell you what it indicates to me. Bad conscience. They don't even have the guts to make a war any more.

Pause.

Darwin Perhaps Madame Aung will tell us the story of the film. This is something I'd be very keen to hear.

Mme Aung I feel the ladies have already . . .

Alice We don't mind.

Susan It's all right. Go ahead. We like the bit in the mental ward.

Mme Aung Ah yes.

Susan Raymond will like it. You got me at the Maudsley, didn't you, dear?

Brock Yes, yes.

Susan That's where he proposed to me. A moment of weakness. Of mine, I mean.

Brock Please, darling. . .

Susan I married him because he reminded me of my father.

Mme Aung Really?

Susan At that point, of course, I didn't realise just what a shit my father was.

Pause.

Alice I'm sorry. She has a sort of psychiatric cabaret.

Susan laughs.

Susan That's very good. And there's something about Suez which . . .

Brock Will you please be quiet?

Pause.

The story of the film.

Mme Aung is embarrassed. It takes her considerable effort to start.

Mme Aung There's a woman . . . who despises her husband . . .

Pause.

Susan Is it getting a little bit chilly in here? October nights. Those poor parachutists. I do know how they feel. Even now. Cities. Fields. Trees. Farms. Dark spaces. Lights. The parachute opens. We descend.

Pause.

Of course, we were comparatively welcome, not always ecstatic, not the Gaullists, of course, but by and large we did make it our business to land in countries where we were wanted. Certainly the men were. I mean, some of the relationships, I can't tell you. I remember a colleague telling me of the heat, of the smell of a particular young girl, the hot wet smell, he said. Nothing since. Nothing since then. I can't see the Egyptian girls somehow . . . no. Not in Egypt now. I mean, there were broken hearts when we left. I mean, there are girls today who mourn Englishmen who died in Dachau, died naked in Dachau, men with whom they had spent a single night. Well.

Pause. The tears are pouring down Susan's face, she can barely speak.

But then . . . even for myself I do like to make a point of sleeping with men I don't know. I do find once you get to know them you usually don't want to sleep with them any more . . .

Brock gets up and shouts at the top of his voice across the room.

Brock Please can you stop, can you stop fucking talking for five fucking minutes on end?

Susan I would stop, I would stop, I would stop fucking talking if I ever heard anyone else say anything worth fucking stopping talking for.

Pause. Then Darwin moves.

Darwin I'm sorry. I apologise. I really must go.

He crosses the room.

Mme Aung Farewell.

Aung We are behind you, sir. There is wisdom in your expedition.

Darwin Thank you.

Aung May I say, sir, these gyps need whipping and you are the man to do it?

Darwin Thank you very much. Madame Aung.

Mme Aung We never really met.

Darwin No. No. We never met, that is true. But perhaps, before I go, I may nevertheless set you right on a point of fact. Ingmar Bergman is not a bloody Norwegian, he is a bloody Swede. (*He nods slightly.*) Good night, everyone.

Darwin goes out. Brock gets up and goes to the door, then turns.

Brock He's going to resign.

Pause.

Susan Isn't this an exciting week? Don't you think? Isn't this thrilling? Don't you think? Everything is up for grabs. At last. We will see some changes. Thank the Lord. Now, there was dinner. I made some more dinner for Leonard. A little ham. And chicken. And some pickles and tomato. And lettuce. And there are a couple of pheasants in the fridge. And I can get twelve bottles of claret from the cellar. Why not?
There is plenty.
Shall we eat again?

AUDIENCE MEMBER *Do you still consider* Plenty *to be one of your best plays?*

It's very difficult for me to answer this question. In my heart, yes. There's a wonderful thing Joseph Heller said, and I'm afraid it's immodestly what I feel. They said to him, 'You've never written anything better than *Catch 22*,' and he said, 'No, but nor has anybody else.'

AUDIENCE MEMBER *You treated Colin Powell very sympathetically in* Stuff Happens. *Was that an artifice for the play, so you could have a good and a bad character?*

I hope the play represents the mystery, the contradiction of Colin Powell. He goes along with policies he doesn't believe in, but he goes along with them because he's the Good Soldier and he'll finally report to the president. I hope that's made clear in the scene in which Bush calls him in. The technique of the play is that it's all based on what I believe to have happened, but obviously I wrote the scenes myself. I do know that Bush called him in because the situation became ridiculous: Bush was pursuing a policy that he wasn't telling his own Secretary of State about. Everyone is angry with Powell – the right because he was insufficiently keen on the policy, and opponents of the war because his resignation is the only thing which could have stopped the invasion. He gets it in the neck from everybody. What I try to do in the play is at least to present Powell's point of view.

AUDIENCE MEMBER *Does it make you cynical when you look back at Suez and then make comparisons with what's happening now?*

Well, the difference with Suez is that a year later the prime minister was gone. The idea that it will be possible to move away from what happened, politically, seems to me very unlikely. There was this extraordinary phrase that Sir Anthony Eden's wife used: she said, 'It seemed as if the

Suez Canal flowed through our drawing room.' I just don't see how the living quarters at Number 10 are not now a map of Iraq. I don't know how you can ever move on from something like that. You have the irony of someone who wants to be Margaret Thatcher, who says his hero is Margaret Thatcher, and yet who now perforce sounds a lot more like John Major. He keeps saying 'Let's draw a line under this,' which I remember as John Major's catch-phrase. I don't see how a line can be drawn under what happened in Iraq. It isn't going to happen.

AUDIENCE MEMBER *You said you'd met a number of former SOE women who had got divorced. Did you meet them and then decide to write the play, or did you meet them for research?*

I'd chosen the subject, and also met a lot of people involved in Black Propaganda. I was very fortunate that I just caught the subject before a lot of the significant people involved in it died. People can't now go to primary sources. Or let's say there are fewer – the official historian of SOE, a first-rate historian called M. R. D. Foot, is still alive. But it would be much harder now to write a play which was directly informed. The reason I wanted to write about the war was that the defining event of my life happened before I was born; I was born two years after it ended. My parents kept saying, 'Can we have some peace now, please, can we just have a little peace?' And I kept thinking, peace from what? Why do you keep asking for peace? Once I understood my father had been in Atlantic convoys, then I began to understand why he wanted peace, but until I reconstructed the war, I couldn't understand my own life. A group of writers of my age all began to examine this subject soon after. Ian McEwan, for instance, a year or two later, started a similar project of aiming to write radically about the war, from a new, less hackneyed perspective.

AUDIENCE MEMBER *Do you plan to take* Stuff Happens *to America?*

I don't know what's going to happen to it; it has twenty-two actors in it so it's a very difficult play to present. As I said earlier about the virtues of a subsidised house, what's so wonderful is that in this theatre now, we're able to do a play with twenty-two people in it. American managers keep saying they want to do it, but they're nervous, of course they are. There was a reading, for instance, at Hartford, Connecticut, about ten days ago, and after it one of the Board members at the public discussion said, 'I think if this is the kind of work we're going to present in this theatre, we should end subsidy to the arts in this country altogether.' I think there's going to be a lot of this in the coming year or two, isn't there? We're heading for a difficult mood, plainly, and it may not be a mood in which people want to lose money on *Stuff Happens*. What's my reaction? It breaks my heart.

AUDIENCE MEMBER *To what degree was your play* Stuff Happens *meant to entertain as well as to inform?*

Completely, but then for myself, I don't find 'entertainment' entertaining. I can't stand entertainment, so I write the kind of play I'd like to go to, which is the kind of play I find entertaining, and tends to be a play with some subject-matter. But I know some people love plays about nothing.

AUDIENCE MEMBER *What were your feelings about the film of* Plenty?

It was difficult for me because Kate Nelligan was so identified with the role. I'd directed the play both here and in New York. Kate and I had worked together four times; she did *Dreams of Leaving*, *Knuckle*, *Licking Hitler* and *Plenty*. She was for a long time, while I was finding my own voice, very much the means by which I found it. You find that in the story of many writers. At the moment, for instance, Aaron Eckhart has become the instrument for Neil LaBute, the means through which he has become a wonderful playwright. It was very hard to face the commercial fact that the only way a film was going to be made was through the intervention of Meryl Streep, who wanted to play Susan Traherne. But Meryl Streep is a very interesting person who used her power, in the ten years or so that she could get films made, to get really good things made. Nobody has ever used that power better or more responsibly than Meryl Streep. She got for instance *Silkwood* made, a wonderful film which wouldn't have been made without her. So the film was difficult for me because I didn't direct it, it wasn't my voice, it wasn't emotionally what it had been for me. But was I pleased that a zonking great Hollywood film of *Plenty* was made? Who would not be? And artistically I thought it was excellent. But was it what the play had been to me? How could it be?

AUDIENCE MEMBER *Did you ever get to see Cate Blanchett play the role for the Almeida, because I know you were in New York at the time?*

I did, I got to see it and I thought it was a fantastic production. I thought what was interesting was that the capacity of the play to upset had not gone at all. Some of the reviews were as hostile as ever. And the public flocked again – whether for Cate or the play you can decide. For some of the critics, time had not gone by. They still don't accept they're wrong. I am not forgiven. This is a grudge fight. It's partly the strength of the woman that certain male critics find unbearable. Jonathan Kent, who directed the revival, is in the audience . . .

JONATHAN KENT *Yes, it was interesting to see that audiences were divided along gender lines. Men tend to not like it and women identify with it.*

There was an interesting thing in Tokyo where it was an enormous success. I asked how come it was such a success, and they said, 'Oh, all the men leave at half time, but all the women stay for the second half, and they stay because there has never been a play about a woman.' I said there must have been productions of *A Streetcar Named Desire*, and they said, 'Yes, but a play where the woman is at the centre of the stage, not a victim.' They said the women didn't mind what the play was, it was just so revolutionary for there to be a woman at the centre of the stage and for it to be about her. It's been interesting. *Plenty*'s not going to settle into a genteel classic.

AUDIENCE MEMBER *With* Stuff Happens, *do you think the play illuminates the American election result, or the election result illuminates the play?*

I think the play is right about something I've been claiming. You can fairly see the play as the story of how the supposedly stupid man often wins over the supposedly clever man. Everyone keeps telling us how stupid George Bush is, but he seems to have come out of the situation quite well. And everyone keeps telling us how clever Tony Blair is, but he seems to have come out of it quite badly. He's got nothing out of it, and Bush has got what he wanted out of it. So the thesis of the play, and particularly in Alex Jennings' wonderful performance, is that cunning of a man who knows he's not intellectually the most devastating person you're ever going to meet, but who nevertheless knows how to use what intelligence he has for cunning ends. I'm afraid to say I always thought Bush would win again, and never for a moment believed he wouldn't. I think the play shows an operator, somebody who knows how to come out on top. I think that's a true-ish portrait of how he is in a room. People who know Bush say it's pretty true to the way he operates. The thing that clinched it for me was the description of how a fifty-five-minute meeting with Bush will be fifty-four minutes of you talking, then him saying, 'Thank you very much, I'll think about it. I'll let you know.' It's a strategy. And it's a strategy that's proving remarkably effective.

AUDIENCE MEMBER *If tomorrow you were given an ultimatum that you could either write only plays or only screenplays, which would you choose?*

Plays. I would miss cinema terribly, but there was a certain point in my life when I had to decide. I reached a fork in the road. It was roughly when I was asked to commit to writing three plays for the National Theatre, in Richard Eyre's day as Director, in the late eighties, early nineties. It was at that moment that an awful lot of people began asking me to write an awful lot of films. I had to make a decision which I've basically stuck with, which was that the theatre is more important to me.

AUDIENCE MEMBER *I wonder which other modern British playwrights you admire?*

I suppose inevitably my own generation, there are certain people whose name on the bill means that I will always go and see their work. I don't think any of us likes every single play by each other, but I'm never going to miss a play by Caryl Churchill, and I'm never going to miss a play by Howard Brenton or Christopher Hampton. Of the Americans, I'm never going to miss Neil LaBute, or Wallace Shawn, who is a special favourite of mine. I'm obviously going to see these plays. Why would I miss them?

AUDIENCE MEMBER *In* Acting Up *you mention a remark of Wallace Shawn's about* Plenty *and political theatre ...*

Yes, Wallace Shawn said it was very unusual to see a play that contains an idea of how you might have lived, as well as a description of how you actually live. Political play-writing doesn't make sense unless it has some sense of how things might be otherwise. If it doesn't contain possibility, then there isn't any point in political writing, whereas a social realist writer doesn't feel that. They just feel happy to describe, and recognition is what they want from the audience, for the audience to say, 'Oh, yes, I know that, that's true.' A political playwright is someone who is defined by a sense of what might be, as well as what is; that argument between what we could be and what we are. When you ask which writers I admire, you always find that, which effectively means a sense of history. You find it in writers like Chekhov, who wouldn't say he was a political writer, but history is sweeping through the room, you can feel it. In Chekhov more than anyone, there is that sense of what we might have been, which is what makes his work so powerful.

AUDIENCE MEMBER *Do you have other plays coming up in the future?*

Totally exhausted! *Stuff Happens* was quite a lot of work, and I've basically had to devote the whole year to thinking about the war.

AUDIENCE MEMBER *Any chance of you reviving another of the big plays you wrote,* Pravda?

We're trying to revive *Pravda* (which I wrote with Howard Brenton), but there is still – and I find this astonishing, and a rebuke to the acting profession – a terror of following Anthony Hopkins in the role of Lambert Le Roux. It seems impossible that a performance can cast a twenty-year shadow, but we find this. If it was said once, one would laugh, but by the time it's been said many times . . . It was a very great performance, it's true, but we'd love to see the play again, Howard and I. It's a play about Murdoch-ism, essentially, and it's only become more pressing.

AUDIENCE MEMBER *You've talked about your work as political drama. Would you say it's satire?*

Well, *Pravda* was a satire. I like writing satire with Howard Brenton. Satire is what you can write with somebody else because it's essentially destructive, at its best. It exists to say 'no' to things. Two people can say 'no' together whereas two people trying to write 'yes' together can be harder, because the things you agree on tend to be negatives whereas the positives are harder to agree on with another writer. It's great fun writing stuff that's just there to make people laugh, as I hope *Pravda* – and *Brassneck*, the other satire Howard and I wrote together – do. But do I think of myself as a satirist? No. I was originally, I started writing satire, and I lost my first agent when I tried to switch from being funny. He thought I was a comic writer and shouldn't waste my time trying to be serious as I wasn't any good at it. That, basically, was why I went to be represented by Peggy Ramsay, who changed my life. In the years before *Plenty*, and while I was writing *Plenty* and *Licking Hitler*, she was the person who made me feel I wasn't a complete fool for writing more serious plays. Or let's say plays with fewer laughs.

AUDIENCE MEMBER *I hope you keep writing about what you find most annoying and what you feel strongly about.*

Well, thank you, that's my intention.

Tom Stoppard

Cast performing the extracts:

Henry Carr Simon Green
Cecily Emma Fielding

CHRISTOPHER CAMPBELL *Twenty-five years ago, I asked
my then headmaster if I could put on a production of*
Travesties *at school. He said, 'What's it about?' So I have
some hope that I'm going to wake up shortly and find myself, aged fifteen and feeling rather smug, having dreamt a
successful conversation on that very topic, with the author.
If not, it's still a pleasure, twenty-five years later. We're
going to start by talking a bit about Faber, in honour of
whose seventy-fifth anniversary this series of interviews
is taking place. I was sent an extract from a forthcoming
history of the company, which says 'From the mid-sixties
there were new names, and an expansion of the drama list.
Editor Frank Pike had approached the features editor of
a Bristol daily paper, who had been a university contem-
porary, asking if he knew of any promising writers. He
suggested one of the paper's journalists, Stoppard. It was
assumed that the young writer would produce prose fiction, and Stoppard did contribute to the* Introduction *series
of new fiction. Subsequently,* Rosencrantz and Guildenstern Are Dead *was a hit at the 1966 Edinburgh Festival
and was lauded by Kenneth Tynan; it was clear that
Stoppard was a dramatist and not a closet novelist.' And
his first play was soon published by Faber. Do you remember your first contact with the company?*

TOM STOPPARD I had forgotten, but he wasn't a features
editor, he had an arts page. This was Anthony Smith, whose
byline is A. C. H. Smith; he was already a poet, and subsequently a novelist and playwright. It's absolutely true,
I remember now. He had been at Cambridge with Frank

Pike, and Anthony suggested me. I think I'd written a couple of short stories, then I wrote another one, and Faber took them for a book called *Introduction 2*. I think *Introduction 1* had Ted Hughes in it. *Introduction 2* had Shena MacKay and half a dozen other writers; and that was the first time I'd been in print, apart from the *Western Daily Press* which, mind you, was also exciting for me at the time.

Did you think, then, that you were a closet novelist at that stage?

I wasn't actually, no. Come to think of it, I only wrote a novel because a publisher, Anthony Blond, suggested that I should write a novel. That seemed to me like a tremendous gift, because in the natural order of things a young writer might produce a novel and hope desperately to interest some publisher. To have a publisher express an interest in a novel which I hadn't written was an offer you couldn't refuse, so I wrote a novel almost to order. But by that time I'd certainly written some plays; I know I'd already done a little sketch of *The Real Inspector Hound*. Many of the audience won't remember this, but back then most people of my sort of age who wanted to write were very attracted to writing plays because a disproportionate amount of interest was paid to the theatre at that period – the middle fifties onwards. We were all, as it were, unproduced playwrights rather than unpublished novelists.

To move on to Travesties: *it was first produced in 1974. Had you written it long before that?*

No, not at all. *Jumpers*, the play before that, was 1972, and I guess I was working on *Travesties* pretty much in the intervening two years.

What was the germ of the play? What first set it going?

Reading Ellmann's biography of James Joyce. *Travesties* is a play with four real live people in it: three of them very well known – Joyce, Lenin and Tristan Tzara. The fourth one is sometimes thought to have been my invention. He wasn't; he was a man called Henry Carr, who was the British Consul or something in Zurich during the First World War. He was involved in an amateur production of *The Importance of Being Earnest* (I'm now just trying to 'platform' the extract a little bit). Joyce played one of the roles, and ended up going to court. There was a rather unseemly litigation about who should pay for Joyce's trousers. This man Henry Carr was, as it were, given to me by Richard Ellmann's biography of Joyce, and I took it from there, really. It's very useful, if you're my kind of writer, to have a protagonist who is a senile fantasist with a bad memory. I was able to do more or less what I liked as it was all happening inside his head. I'll add a postscript to that of some interest. I was absolutely dumbfounded, slightly horrified, one day, after the play had been around for a little bit, to receive a letter from Henry Carr's widow, at a point in my life when I'd forgotten that I hadn't invented him. She came to see the play and she gave John Wood, who played Henry Carr, Henry's actual cigarette case. The whole thing was unbearably moving.

Was she happy with the portrayal?

I think she took the point that it wasn't exactly a portrayal, but she seemed very happy with the event.

You mentioned the other three real characters in the play, and that they are extremely well known. Were you conscious at the time of the audacity of putting those three on stage? People constantly try to put literary geniuses into plays and are then stuck with the problem of making them sound as if they are literary geniuses. Did you just know you could do that or were you worried at all?

I wasn't worried, because I was young and it wasn't really I who put them together. The point is that Lenin, Joyce and Tristan Tzara were all in Zurich at the same time. If I'd been more ambitious, there were one or two other people I might have potted. It was a kind of gift, if you think about it. The Dadaist, the Bolshevik, and the author of *Ulysses*, all involved in certain real events such as the production of *The Importance of Being Earnest*. It was all coming at me, too much, too rich, really. I think I had a nice time living with the play.

You're quite right to point out that this was a real conjunction, but many people would say this was a quintessentially Stoppardian collection of people to put in a play. Do you think Stoppardian is a word with any meaning, or just a lazy way of saying 'awfully clever'?

In my real life, my personal and domestic life, Stoppardian has come to mean a kind of minor domestic catastrophe – putting the milk into the dishwasher is Stoppardian, for example. I'd love to be somebody who had given an adjective to the language, but alas, essentially I think it doesn't really operate in that way.

Very well. So shall we hear the extract?

This is Henry Carr himself, in his imagination, involved with a young woman working in the Zurich reference library. Her education has been very methodical, in fact it's been alphabetical. He purports to have had a similar kind of education, based on alphabetical precedence. *Travesties* was a very strange text in a way. Some of it's in limerick form; a lot of it is not exactly a pastiche of *The Importance of Being Earnest* but something which tries to hit off the tone of that play. Then there's a kind of documentary section involving Lenin trying to get to the Finland Station in 1917. The writing was quite arch in some sense. Perhaps I shouldn't try to apologise for it in advance . . .

Cecily sees Carr, who hands her the visiting card he received from Bennett in Act One.

Cecily Tristan Tzara. Dada, Dada, Dada . . . *Why, it's Jack's younger brother!!*

Carr You must be Cecily!

Cecily Ssssh!

Carr You are!

Cecily And you, I see from your calling card, are Jack's decadent nihilist younger brother.

Carr Oh, I'm not really a decadent nihilist at all, Cecily. You mustn't think that I am a decadent nihilist.

Cecily If you are not then you have certainly been deceiving us all in a very inexcusable manner. To *masquerade* as a decadent nihilist – or at any rate to ruminate in different colours and display the results in the Bahnhofstrasse – would be hypocritical.

Carr (*taken aback*) Oh! Of course, I have been rather *louche* and devil-take-the-hindmost.

Cecily I am glad to hear it.

Carr In fact now you mention the subject I have made quite a corner in voluptuous disdain.

Cecily I don't think you should be so proud of it, however pleasant it must be. You have been a great disappointment to your brother.

Carr Well, my brother has been a great disappointment to me, and to Dada. His mother isn't exactly mad about him either. My brother Jack is a booby, and if you want to know why he is a booby, I will tell you why he is a booby. He told me that you were rather pretty, whereas

35

you are at a glance the prettiest girl in the whole world. Have you got any books here one can borrow?

Cecily I don't think you ought to talk to me like that during library hours. However, as the reference section is about to close for lunch I will overlook it. Intellectual curiosity is not so common that one can afford to discourage it. What kind of books were you wanting?

Carr Any kind at all.

Cecily Is there no limit to the scope of your interests?

Carr It is rather that I wish to increase it. An overly methodical education has left me to fend as best I can with some small knowledge of the aardvark, a mastery of the abacus and a facility for abstract art. An aardvark, by the way, is a sort of African pig found mainly –

Cecily I know only too well what an aardvark is, Mr Tzara. To be frank, you strike a sympathetic chord in me.

Carr Politically, I haven't really got beyond anarchism.

Cecily I see. Your elder brother, meanwhile –

Carr Bolshevism. And you, I suppose . . . ?

Cecily Zimmervaldism!

Carr Oh, Cecily, will you not make it your mission to reform me? We can begin over lunch. It will give me an appetite. Nothing gives me an appetite so much as renouncing my beliefs over a glass of hock.

Cecily I'm afraid I am too busy to reform you today. I must spend the lunch hour preparing references for Lenin.

Carr Some faithful governess seeking fresh pastures?

Cecily Far from it. I refer to Vladimir Ilyich who with my little help is writing his book on *Imperialism: the Highest Stage of Capitalism*.

Carr Of course – *Lenin*. But surely, now that the revolution has broken out in St Petersburg, he will be anxious to return home?

Cecily That is true. When the history of the Revolution – or indeed of anything else – is written, Switzerland is unlikely to loom large in the story. However, all avenues are closed to him. He will have to travel in disguise with false papers. Oh, but I fear I have said too much already. Vladimir is positive that there are agents watching him and trying to ingratiate themselves with those who are close to him. The British are among the most determined, though the least competent. Only yesterday the Ambassador received secret instructions to watch the ports.

Carr (*ashamed*) The ports?

Cecily At the same time, the Consul in Zurich has received a flurry of cryptic telegrams suggesting intense and dramatic activity – 'Knock 'em cold' – 'Drive 'em Wilde' – 'Break a leg' – and one from the Ambassador himself, 'Thinking of you tonight, Horace.'

Carr I think I can throw some light on that. The Consul has been busy for several weeks in rehearsals which culminated last evening in a performance at the Theater zur Kaufleuten on Pelikanstrasse. I happened to be present.

Cecily That would no doubt explain why he virtually left the Consulate's affairs in the hands of his manservant – who, fortunately, has radical sympathies.

Carr Good heavens!

Cecily You seem surprised.

Carr Not at all. I have a servant myself.

Cecily I am afraid that I disapprove of servants.

Carr You are quite right to do so. Most of them are without scruples.

Cecily In the socialist future, no one will have any.

Carr So I believe. To whom did this manservant pass the Consul's correspondence?

Cecily Your brother Jack. Oh dear, there I go again! You are not a bit like your brother. You are more English.

Carr I assure you I am as Bulgarian as he is.

Cecily He is Romanian.

Carr They are the same place. Some people call it the one, some the other.

Cecily I didn't know that, though I always suspected it.

Carr Anyway, now that *Earnest* has opened, no doubt the Consul will relieve his servant of diplomatic business. In all fairness, he did have a personal triumph in a most demanding role.

Cecily *Earnest*?

Carr No – the other one.

Cecily What do you mean by *Earnest*?

Carr *The Importance of Being Earnest* by Oscar Wilde.

Cecily Wilde?

Carr You know him?

Cecily No, in literature I am only up to G. But I've heard of him and I don't like him. The life is the art, as Vladimir Ilyich always says.

Carr *Ars longa, vita brevis*, Cecily.

Cecily Let us leave his proclivities in the decent obscurity of a learned tongue, Mr Tzara. I was referring to the fact that Oscar Wilde was a bourgeois individualist and, so I hear, overdressed from habit to boot.

Carr From habit to boot?

Cecily And back again.

Carr He may occasionally have been a little over-dressed but he made up for it by being immensely uncommitted.

Cecily The sole duty and justification for art is social criticism.

Carr That is a most interesting view of the sole duty and justification for art, Cecily, but it has the disadvantage that a great deal of what we call art has no such function and yet in some way it gratifies a hunger that is common to princes and peasants.

Cecily In an age when the difference between prince and peasant was thought to be in the stars, Mr Tzara, art was naturally an affirmation for the one and a consolation to the other; but we live in an age when the social order is seen to be the work of material forces, and we have been given an entirely new kind of responsibility, the responsibility of changing society.

Carr No, no, no, no, no – my dear girl! – art doesn't change society, it is merely changed by it.

From here the argument becomes gradually heated.

Cecily Art is a critique of society or it is nothing!

Carr Do you know Gilbert and Sullivan?!

Cecily I know Gilbert but not Sullivan.

Carr Well, if you knew *Iolanthe* like I know *Iolanthe* –

Cecily I doubt it –

Carr *Patience*!

Cecily How dare you!

Carr *Pirates*! *Pinafore*!

Cecily Control yourself!

Carr *Ruddigore*!

Cecily This is a Public Library, Mr Tzara!

Carr *GONDOLIERS*, madam!

Another 'time slip' . . .

Cecily I don't think you ought to talk to me like that during library hours. However, as the reference section is about to close for lunch I will overlook it. Intellectual curiosity is not so common that one can afford to discourage it. What kind of books were you wanting?

Carr Any kind at all. You choose. I should like you, if you would, to make it your mission to reform me. We can begin over lunch.

Cecily I'm afraid I am too busy to reform you today. You will have to reform yourself. Here is an article which I have been translating for Vladimir Ilyich. You may not be aware, Mr Tzara, that in the governments of Western Europe today there are ten Socialist ministers.

Carr I must admit my work has prevented me from taking an interest in European politics. But ten is certainly impressive.

Cecily It is scandalous. They are supporting an imperialist war. Meanwhile the real struggle, the class war, is being undermined by these revisionists like Kautsky and MacDonald.

Carr (*puzzled*) Do you mean Ramsay MacDonald, Cecily?

Cecily I don't mean Flora Macdonald, Mr Tzara.

Carr But he's an absolute Bolshie.

Cecily He is working within the bourgeois capitalist system and postponing its destruction. Karl Marx has shown that capitalism is digging its own grave.

Carr No, no, no, no, my dear girl – Marx got it wrong. He got it wrong for good reasons but he got it wrong just the same. By bad luck he encountered the capitalist system at its most deceptive period. The industrial revolution had crowded the people into slums and enslaved them in factories, but it had not yet begun to bring them the benefits of an industrialised society. Marx drew the lesson that the wealth of the capitalist had been stolen from the worker in the form of unpaid labour. He thought that was how the whole thing worked. That false premise was itself added to a false assumption. Marx assumed that people would behave according to their class. But they didn't. In all kinds of ways and for all kinds of reasons, the classes moved closer together instead of further apart. The critical moment never came. It receded. The tide must have turned at about the time when *Das Kapital* after eighteen years of hard labour was finally coming off the press, a moving reminder, Cecily, of the folly of authorship. How sweet you look suddenly – pink as a rose.

Cecily That's because I'm about to puke into your nancy straw hat, you *prig*! – you swanking canting fop, you bourgeois intellectual humbugger, you – artist! Marx warned us against the liberals, the philanthropists, the piecemeal reformers – change won't come from *them* but from a head-on collision, *that's* how history works! When Lenin was twenty-one there was famine in Russia. The intellectuals organised relief – soup kitchens, seed corn, all kinds of do-gooding with Tolstoy in the lead. Lenin did – nothing. He understood that the famine was a force for the revolution. Twenty-one years old, in

Samara, in 1890–91. He was a boy, and he understood that, so don't talk to me about superior morality, you patronising Kant-struck prig, all the time you're talking about the classes you're trying to imagine how I'd look stripped off to my knickers –

Carr That's a lie!

> *But apparently it isn't. As Cecily continues to speak we get a partial Carr's-mind view of her. Coloured lights begin to play over her body, and most of the other light goes except for a bright spot on Carr.*

> *Faintly, from 1974, comes the sound of a big band playing 'The Stripper'. Carr is in a trance. The music builds. Cecily might perhaps climb on to her desk. The desk may have 'cabaret lights' built into it for use at this point.*

Cecily The only way is the way of Marx and of Lenin, the enemy of all revisionism! – of opportunist liberal economism! – of social-chauvinist bourgeois individualism! – quasi-Dadaist paternalism! – pseudo-Wildean aphorism! – sub-Joycean catechism and dogmatism! – cubism! – expressionism! – rheumatism! –

Carr *Get 'em off!*

> *The light snaps back to normal.*

Cecily I don't think you ought to talk to me like that during library hours. However, as the reference section is about to close for lunch I will overlook it. Intellectual curiosity is not so common that one can afford to discourage it. What kind of books were you wanting?

Carr Books? What books? What do you mean, Cecily, by books? I have read Mr Lenin's article and I don't need to read any more. I have come to tell you that you seem to me to be the visible personification of absolute perfection.

Cecily In body or mind?

Carr In every way.

Cecily Oh, Tristan!

Carr You will love me back and tell me all your secrets, won't you?

Cecily You silly boy! Of course! I have waited for you for months.

Carr (*amazed*) For months?

Cecily Ever since Jack told me he had a younger brother who was a decadent nihilist it has been my girlish dream to reform you and to love you.

Carr Oh, Cecily!

Her embrace drags him down out of sight behind her desk. He resurfaces momentarily –

Carr But, my dear Cecily, you don't mean that you couldn't love me if –

– and is dragged down again.

During the extract, I suddenly remembered that when she starts going into that speech, in the first production, she was standing on her library desk and electric light chasers were going round the desk while she took her clothes off. I'm not saying we should necessarily have done that this afternoon . . .

When you listen to that, from a play you wrote some years ago, do you think 'Oh yes,' or 'Oh no'?

I felt pleased but quite critical. As a matter of fact, just now and again it illustrated something which I was going to refer to, which is why I'm clutching something here. Now and again I could see that I'd got quite pleased with what I'd found out and insisted on telling the audience what it was that I had found out whether they wanted to know it or not. So all kinds of historical details crept in which one might have snipped a little bit, but on the whole I thought it was OK. There was a page-long speech which I much later let a chap have for a little magazine. I thought I'd read it to you. Writing the speech and then cutting it from the play before it was ever performed, was an instance of something which perhaps many playwrights learn secretly and don't talk about very much. It was an instance of that moment of learning that because something is true it doesn't necessarily mean that it's interesting. If you're writing about real events and real people on whatever level, one becomes quite attached to the fruits of one's investigation and sometimes insists on putting them up here, when they don't really wear very well.

I'll read it because it might as well have a moment of glory at the National Theatre which it would never otherwise have. And what I will say to you is that every single fact and name in this speech is historically authentic, and the speaker is James Joyce, talking to Tzara.

Joyce My father sometimes wore a monocle. I think I recall it as far back as Castlewood Avenue, which we left when I was five. Also in Martello Terrace, our house in Bray; also in Carrisfort Avenue, Black Rock; and without doubt in Fitzgibbon Street, Number 14, off Mountjoy Street, our last good address which we vacated in 1894, my thirteenth year. (*It's just showing off.*) Now, let me see, Alderman McCann, whose son was educated with me by the Jesuits at Clongowes; Clancy and Kennedy, among others, at University College; also Courtney of *The Fortnightly Review*, who paid me twelve guineas in 1900 for my review of Ibsen; also Signor Bellini, tenor

with the Carl Rosa Opera Company, who stayed at Finn's
Hotel, where my Nora made the beds before I took her
in my embrace and flew her towards the sun; also Count
Sordina, my English pupil in Trieste; also my friend
Budgen, an artist, blown like me to Zurich; and others
too numerous to mention, all at one time or another have
worn the monocle. On the other hand, the man I once
talked to in the Imperial Hotel in Cork had a glass eye.
We never lived in Cork, but my father came from there
and when he took me with him on a visit in connection
with the sale of property, he was twenty-one. My father
owned, on the death of his father, properties in Cork
bringing in over £300 per annum, and in 1870 £300 was
worth £300. In that same year, he received from his
grandfather, John O'Connell, £1,000 on his coming of
age, and when I tell you that in 1874, his mother's first
cousin, Peter Paul McSwiney, was Lord Mayor of Dublin,
(*Shut up, Tom!*) you will understand that my father could
carry off a monocle with the best of them, and I never
knew him at his best. In 1880, as a member of the Home
Rule Sodality, he was secretary of the United Liberal Club
and in the election that year his efforts unseated the last
two Conservative members for Dublin, Sir Arthur
Guinness, a brewer, and James Stone. My father received
100 guineas from each of the two successful Liberal
candidates and, prompted by a leading article in *The
Freeman's Journal*, the Lord Lieutenant assigned to him
in gratitude a post in the office of the Collector of Rates
at £500 per annum. He got married a month later, and
between 1882 (*and it goes on: 'We stayed here, we stayed
there . . .'*) On the other hand, Billy Boyle, the bicycle
racer, wore a black eyepatch ever since coming to grief in
the downhill event in the Isle of Man. All in all, I am no
stranger to monocularity, Mr Tzara, but I have yet to
meet a man to touch you for two-dimensional vision.

Peter Wood, who directed the first production of *Travesties*, said there was a speech missing. I was going on holiday with my family, and while I was on holiday I ended up writing that speech. I brought it back very proudly, and as soon as I got into rehearsal, it bit the dust.

Yes, I get absolutely enthralled by the period of reading up things, almost to the point of catastrophe. I was actually completely addicted to the reading I was doing for *The Coast of Utopia*, and in the end I had to will myself to stop, to start writing before it was too late.

I was very surprised, when reading Travesties *again recently, to be reminded so much of your other and subsequent work.*

Really?

Well that group of emigrés in a foreign city immediately made me think of Coast of Utopia, *and* The Invention of Love *with the old man and young man appearing in the same play. Those things I didn't realise were enduring themes to your work, but there they were.*

AUDIENCE MEMBER *I had the good fortune of seeing* Jumpers *in New York three times, and wondered what you thought of how it was put on there?*

As a matter of fact I thought it sat better on that stage than in London – this is entirely a matter of the relationship between the auditorium and the height of the stage. It worked well. Simon Russell Beale playing George is a pretty good start, isn't it? And I thought Essie Davis was a wonderful Dottie, so it was pleasing, yes.

AUDIENCE MEMBER *David Hare was rather hostile to the critics in a previous talk in this series. What is your attitude to critics?*

I don't feel hostility. It's a very strange profession, it's a difficult thing to do, I think. Sports critics don't understand a football match or a cricket match unless they've played the game. Even after many years, theatre critics sometimes fail to understand why they like something and why they don't like something else. The only thing I think is slightly worrying about critics is that they're beginning to follow a certain kind of American film criticism where they're essentially doing thumbs-up-thumbs-down reviewing. I've begun to notice that a particular critic (and there's no need or point in saying which one) for whom everything is absolutely unbelievably wonderful, or completely and utterly awful. And actually theatre, life, simply isn't like that. The whole tendency towards polarity is something to which you could say I'm hostile. Hostile to an inclination, a tendency, rather than to critics as such.

AUDIENCE MEMBER *Tristan Tzara in* Travesties *makes a poem by drawing words out of a hat. Can a playwright do that?*

What Tzara actually does is to cut up a Shakespeare sonnet into individual words and then draw them randomly from his hat, a pretty authentic and not uninteresting Dadaist practice. I couldn't possibly rely on chance because chance wouldn't provide what I want if I had all the words on the desk and was moving them round to try and get the sort of sequence which, by surreal accident, made some kind of point. So the answer is you cannot draw that page out of your hat. You won't get what you want.

AUDIENCE MEMBER *Do you have a favourite play among your own?*

Not exactly that. I have plays which have been luckier than others, they sort of worked out, so – I know this sounds a bit strange – one feels a kind of fond gratitude towards some plays rather than others. Latterly, by which I mean in the last decade or two, I've tried not to know too much about where I'm going, rather than doing all the worrying up front and sorting everything out – this will be the first act curtain, then Jones will come in and shoot Smith. Now I try just to feel my way forward more, and the consequence is that if things work out for you, you don't feel clever, you feel lucky, and one should always respond with fond gratitude to one's luck. *Travesties* is quite a lucky play. I know that I had no idea how to finish it. I didn't know the last two lines of the play, I was writing my way towards them, and they just fell off the end of the pen at that moment.

We're going to hear those lines in a moment.

Is that so? I actually meant the last bit of Henry Carr's monologue.

It's the very last duologue we're going to hear, when the two of them are in their eighties.

I'm wrong about it being the last line of the play, then.

I've just corrected Tom Stoppard on his own work!

Have you a copy of the play? Oh, I see what you mean. It is the monologue which follows the duologue. You're going to include that, are you? So we were both right.

AUDIENCE MEMBER *Do you have any project on at the moment?*

A project? Well there are three or four areas of interest, topics, whatever . . . I'm trying to write a play which somehow takes off from these little bits of Lego. I had a go a few weeks ago, and it just wouldn't go. I shall next week have another go. I suppose that's a project, yes. I have to tell you, I got really depressed. I took all my stuff to the place where I work – I'd collected a suitcase full of press cuttings, and I had lots of books – all stuff about things I was beginning to focus on. I cheerfully went off and had a quick read through everything, then thought, 'That's enough of this reading, just get on with it now.' I took the cap off my pen, as it were pressed the starter button, and absolutely nothing happened. A week later I came home again feeling really neurotic about this, thinking, 'That's it. It's over.' Then I had this fantastic breakthrough where it occurred to me that there was absolutely no necessity for me to write a play at all. I cheered up immediately and I've been in the state of cheerfulness ever since.

AUDIENCE MEMBER *Write a play!*

Public pressure . . .

AUDIENCE MEMBER *You mentioned you don't rely too much on chance. Could you just discuss briefly what you think the themes of* Rosencrantz and Guildenstern *are?*

Are you writing a thesis?

AUDIENCE MEMBER *I'm just curious.*

My answer to the question would only be a retrospective look at the play to try to identify a theme or two. Because one thing which is *not* the case is that a play is written to express or illustrate a theme. That's not how it works. The language which I understand as a writer is that *Rosencrantz and Guildenstern Are Dead* is about two courtiers at Elsinore. In other words, I can answer the question in a way that you don't need me to tell you. The theme thing is much more subjective than you think, that is to say that it's in you as much as in me. I think that, like many plays, perhaps like most art, it is susceptible to different kinds of interpretation which do not contradict each other. It's actually more like a complementarity.

Is that story true, about your being asked what is Rosencrantz and Guildenstern Are Dead *about?*

Yes, it is true, and I'm really sorry, Chris, that you had to bring this up.

I'm not going to tell the story. I just wanted to know if it's true.

Well, you can't leave the poor things hanging there . . .

Would you like to, or shall I?

Well, essentially, two or three times in the course of the last god-knows-how-many years, I've said something which I've then lived to regret for ever after. This was actually in New York. The play was done in London in the spring of 1967; I think by the very same autumn we were in New York doing it. I'd had my fill of people asking me what it was about, and at a certain point a woman on a pavement, I think it was actually outside the theatre, said 'What is your play about?' and I rather snapped at her, 'It's about to make me rich.'

That was worth hearing, I think.

Well, it was OK for that moment, but I didn't know she was a journalist. And that quote has come up every year, ever since. I have to say it's unusual in one respect: I did say it.

AUDIENCE MEMBER *Do you have a favourite production of* Travesties?

You have no conception of the difficulty you put a writer in by asking such a question in public. Without its being a value judgement about different people, the fact is that very often one is fondest of the first one for a number of contingent reasons. As it happens, in that case, the main chap [John Wood], was a good friend of mine, and I'd written the play for him, so there were a lot of circumstances which made it a happy occasion.

Old Carr dances back on stage with Old Cecily. Old Cecily is about eighty, of course, like Old Carr. They dance a few decrepit steps.

Old Cecily No, no, no, no, it's pathetic though there was a court case I admit, and your trousers came into it, I don't deny, but you never got close to Vladimir Ilyich, and I don't remember the other one. I do remember Joyce, yes you are quite right and he was Irish with glasses but that was the year after – 1918 – and the train had long gone from the station! I waved a red hanky and cried long live the revolution as the carriage took him away in his bowler hat and yes, I said yes when you asked me, but he was the leader of millions by the time you did your Algernon . . .

Carr Algernon – that was him.

Old Cecily I said that was the year after –

Carr After what?

Old Cecily You never even saw Lenin.

Carr Yes I did. Saw him in the cafés. I knew them all. Part of the job.

Old Cecily And you were never the Consul.

Carr Never said I was.

Old Cecily Yes you did.

Carr Should we have a cup of tea?

Old Cecily The Consul was Percy somebody.

Carr (Bennett.)

Old Cecily What?

Carr (*testily*) I said the Consul's name was Bennett!

Old Cecily Oh yes . . . Bennett . . . That's another thing –

Carr Are we going to have a cup of tea or not?

Old Cecily And I never helped him write *Imperialism: the Highest Stage of Capitalism*. That was the year before, too. 1916.

Carr Oh, Cecily. I wish I'd known then that you'd turn out to be a pedant! (*getting angry*) Wasn't this – Didn't do that – 1916 – 1917 – *What of it?* I was here. They were here. They went on. I went on. We all went on.

Old Cecily No, we didn't. We stayed. Sophia married that artist. I married you. You played Algernon. They all went on.

Most of the fading light is on Carr now.

Carr Great days . . . Zurich during the war. Refugees, spies, exiles, painters, poets, writers, radicals of all kinds. I knew them all. Used to argue far into the night . . . at the Odeon, the Terrasse . . . I learned three things in Zurich during the war. I wrote them down. Firstly, you're either a revolutionary or you're not, and if you're not you might as well be an artist as anything else. Secondly, if you can't be an artist, you might as well be a revolutionary . . . I forget the third thing.

Blackout.

So those were the lines you were referring to?

That's right.

Tony Harrison

16 NOVEMBER 2004
COTTESLOE THEATRE

Cast performing the extracts:

Silenus Barrie Rutter
Grenfell Tony Harrison

PAUL ALLEN *Tony Harrison is not a poet and something else, he's not a poet and critic, poet and novelist, or poet and belle lettriste. He's a poet full stop. He's especially not a poet and playwright. He's a poet in the theatre. The fifth volume of his plays has just been published by Faber. The word unique is not to be used lightly, and is nearly always used wrongly, but if anyone else knows of a writer currently working successfully and directly in the theatre as a poet, I'd be interested to hear about it. You've arrived in this position, but it's been by a circuitous route . . .*

TONY HARRISON It was a very circuitous route. Even when I was very small, and knew I was a poet, I also wanted to be a poet in the theatre. Unfortunately, partly to do with the nineteenth-century poets only imitating Shakespeare and making very book-bound, non-theatrical poetry, and then – and I hate to be critical of one of the great spirits of Faber and Faber who are presiding over this event and have done wonderful things but – T. S. Eliot, who was a great poet, was not a great dramatist. He somehow left a climate where people didn't want poets anywhere near the theatre. This is sad because, in his early interest in the theatre, he started being inspired by popular theatre; he's got an Aristophanic fragment which is very interesting, he was interested in Marie Lloyd, in ballet, in Japanese theatre. But he eventually settled into a kind of drawing-room drama which was the death of English theatre. I had to find another route into it because the great tradition of European theatre, for two thousand years or more, is of poets working directly with actors, poets writing plays in verse for actors, performers that they knew. I wanted to have this, but didn't know how to do it. There was no welcome for a poet in the theatre, partly because of Eliot and Fry's legacy. So what I had to do was to go sideways and, because I'd been passionate about learning languages, tap into the classical traditions, translate some of the great poetic dramatists and clear a space for myself. That's how I started working at the National Theatre, in 1973, when I did *The Misanthrope* of Molière.

Molière is quite a far cry from the classical Greek territory that you adopted later and which is going to be significant tonight. I'm interested in how, when you're tapping into different cultures in this way, you make them somehow your own voice. I don't know that Molière spoke with a Leeds accent ...

And I didn't do my version in a Leeds accent. The theme of accent does appear in my work and it's partly because I had a very strong South Leeds accent as a child. I started learning Greek, at the age of eleven, with a thick Yorkshire accent. I wasn't allowed to read poetry at school because of my accent, so something in this little boy said, 'Right you buggers, I am going to write my own poetry in my own voice.' That's true of my own poetry, and it's true of the reclamation I did of the mediaeval plays, the *Mysteries*. When I saw them as a child, God and Jesus spoke in posh Southern RP voices, and only the comic roles had a local accent. I was fired up to reclaim them for northen actors, which I did in this theatre. It was also part of the journey which led into *The Oresteia*, which was also very northern, for other reasons.

Bringing us on to The Oresteia, *what were the reasons for making that sound with your voice in that way?*

The thing about writing for the theatre is that it's a great relief. I write my poetry in my own voice, and I'm usually very disappointed when I hear an actor read my poems on that *Poetry Please* programme on the BBC. I find it dreadful. But I write *plays* for other voices. To imagine other voices is one of the great liberations; you can start using a vocabulary that you wouldn't use in your own voice. *The Misanthrope* opened at the Old Vic in February 1973; in that March I had a meeting with Peter Hall and we decided to do *The Oresteia*, but it wasn't until 1981 that we did it, so I had a long time to think about it. The reason I used northern voices was also to make a connection between the epic world of the *Iliad* and the Homeric world and Aeschylus. The work of Aeschylus is said to be 'slices from the banquet of Homer'. I looked for a heroic world in our own culture, and it's Anglo-Saxon. The world of alliterative Anglo-Saxon poetry stayed longer in the North, so I used an alliterative Anglo-Saxon metric and northern voices.

You do generally vary the metre quite a lot, in the way the great writers did. We think of the iambic as the natural form, and I guess it is, but they also used very elaborate metres in the choruses.

They had an iambic metre like ours, but it's more long-and-short, crotchet-and-quaver than ours, which is more based on stress. I like to vary the metre as they did. Something else came out of *The Oresteia*. In this theatre there are three auditoriums and I've worked in all of them. There are three companies and lots of people milling around. We got a lot of flak on *The Oresteia* for having, for archaeological reasons, a cast of all men, in masks, with this strong alliterative metre. You can't understand Greek drama without remembering that in a day at the ancient festivals there were three tragedies, plus a satyr play. After these tragedies, on came these half-men, half-goats, with enormous erect phalluses, and did a kind of parody version of the themes you had seen before, and restored people full of the tragic experience to their sensual, physical selves. So I thought I should do a satyr play, and I said to the women in the company that one day I would write a play in which I'd reverse men playing women and have women playing men, but I said maybe you could do a satyr play to comment on the overpowering masculinity of *The Oresteia*. It never happened, but it led me into writing the play, *The Trackers of Oxyrhynchus*.

After you'd had three tragedies that have really put the audience through an emotional mangle, does the satyr play say, 'It's all right, we'll have a bit of fun now'?

No, I think it's more restoring the spectators to themselves as sentient, physical, sensual beings. We can have all kinds of intellectual terrors but we still feel hungry, we still want sex. It reminds people of this dimension of themselves. It seems to me a very important part of the Greek tragic vision; you can't understand it without this. But there are almost no satyr plays remaining. There's only one fully complete one – the *Cyclops* of Euripides. I looked at these fragments of *The Trackers,* the *Ichneutae* of Sophocles, then made a play about the two Oxford papyrologists, Grenfell and Hunt, who discovered the fragments in the deserts of Egypt, at a place called Behnesa. I've been there, in fact I took the published Faber text of *The Trackers of Oxyrhynchus* back to the rubbish heaps of Oxyrhynchus and buried it after the play had been done. On these rubbish tips, about 120 miles south of Cairo, on the Nile, the desert preserved these papyri, and among them, in 1907, were discovered fragments of plays. So I made my play out of that discovery, and the transformation of the people who discovered it, into the play itself.

Maybe I should read a bit. I'm not one of those people who sit and write a script then look for a theatre, a director and actors. I like to write a little bit then find the actor who will commit to doing it, and then, when I know who

I'm writing for, I write the play. I wrote Grenfell/Apollo for
Jack Shepherd, and Hunt/Silenus for Barrie [Rutter].

Somewhere in the rubbish heaps there's Sophocles,
Euripides, there may be Homer. The Fellaheen, the local
Egyptians, were using this stuff, as it's the only organic
material in the desert, as compost for their cabbages.

Grenfell

These chaps, our Fellaheen, can't see what's unique
about scraps of old papyri in ancient Greek.
We ship back papyri and decipher them at Queen's
but the natives used to use them as compost for their
    greens!
These treasures of a soul-enriching ancient tongue
shovelled on to barrows and used like so much dung!
Just imagine Homer, Sophocles and Plato
used as compost for the carrot and potato.
They even burn papyrus for the fragrance it releases
and fumigate their fetid tents with long-lost
    masterpieces!

Papyri! Insects gnaw them. Time corrodes
and native plants get potted in a mulch of Pindar's Odes.
Horrible to contemplate! How can a person sleep
while Sophocles is rotting on an ancient rubbish heap!

Here at Oxyrhynchus our present excavation 's
lived up to and surpassed all expectations.
Crate after crate shipped off, load after load
from laundry list and ledger work to tragedy and ode.
Though I'm peeved to report so far this expedition 's
pretty short on poetry but piles up these petitions.

Grenfell becomes Apollo and Hunt becomes Silenus. Apollo
has lost his cattle and the satyr trackers offer to track them
down, and they discover Hermes has made the first lyre

in the history of civilisation out of the skin of the cattle of Apollo and a tortoise. They hear the sound: 'It's very spooky – must be the prototype of the bazouki.' Then Silenus comes on and encourages his troops:

Silenus
You're pathetic. You're all made of jelly.
Every man-beast of you 's a yeller-belly.
You cowardly creeps, you dastardly dogs,
you're not fit to buckle or bull up my clogs.
The buzz of a few lobelia-browsing bees
has you lot trembling at the knees.
Some shepherd's yell, some midget poodle's yap,
and your clogs are all clarted with panicker's crap.
Unmanned, un*horsed* by some moggy's meek miaou
made into cowards by one moo from a cow.

And if that sound had the merest hint of moo
it might be the herd these tracks have led to.
Scared of your own shadow, no spunk, no spine,
all talk and tupping, no true sons of mine.
Bragging and shagging, that's your style,
but show you real action and you run a mile.
You say you'll stick by me, but come the crunch
you turn out such a yeller-bellied bunch.

But Silenus in his day, he never fled.
He faced all dangers with no shred of dread.
Silenus the Satyr, never short of spunk,
braved every battle, never did a bunk.
He was a warrior, valorous, not weak,
not thrown in a panic by a mere squawk or squeak.
When fierce battle raged I never quit –
there I was always in the thick of it.
A hero with honour from many a campaign,
an honour your cowardice will now stain.

Think of an old soldier having to see
his own battalion turn tail and flee.
The ones he brags about as his 'brave boys'
ready to desert the field because of a mere noise,
some squawk, some squeak, some tu-whit-tu-whoo.
A fieldmouse's fart 's enough to scare you.
Fabled as I am for many a noble feat
it breaks this soldier's heart to see you in retreat.

You'd piss off if you heard a parrot sneeze.

*You have to imagine Barrie as he appears on the front of
the NT text, with a very large belly and an even larger
phallus swinging between his knees ... You also tied into
the play petitions on behalf of the homeless, didn't you?
People had probably arrived at the Olivier by walking
from Waterloo Station through the big underpass, which
was then known as cardboard city.*

It was, it was full of people sleeping in cartons. As I said,
you can't understand the tragedy without the satyr play;
and in a way you can't play the satyr play without making
clear the tragedy. What happens in the play, when the
fragments peter out, Apollo gets the lyre and plays the first
lyrical music in civilisation. Before that, satyrs had only
rhythm – they were half-men, half-goats, and in the production we had the hoof part represented by clogs; there
was some wonderful choreography done by Lawrence
Evans. Then melody came into the world, and when the
satyrs hear Apollo playing the first arpeggios on the lyre,
they are entranced and want to play on it themselves. He
says,'No. Get off, you're just meant to dance like animals.
This isn't part of your world.' And he summons up all the
high cultural temples of Europe, including the theatre we
were playing in, the Olivier. Then they get their rewards of
gold bars – they were 'ghetto-blasters' wrapped in gold

paper. As they look at them, I bring in the other story about
satyrs I've always been haunted by – of the satyr Marsyas
who challenged Apollo. Apollo played his lyre and Marsyas
played his flute, and of course he lost the competition
because it was rigged. Apollo played on his lyre, or in some
paintings on the violin, while Marsyas was skinned alive
as punishment for his presumption. I wrote a long speech
for Silenus, suddenly pulling the rug of the comedy away
and showing the divisions between high and low art which
had been created.

Silenus

That's Marsyas screaming! They ripped off his skin
and all he ever wanted was to join in.
Marsyas suffered his terrible flaying
for a bit of innocent *aulos* playing.

The *aulos*, Athene's flute. She flung it away
so why shouldn't Marsyas pick it up and play?
A few blows and the goddess gave the flute
she'd just invented the elegant boot.
She flung the thing aside. Do you know why?
Well, think of the *aulos*. Ever had a try?
You puff your cheeks out, like this, when you play
and she didn't like her face to look that way.
She thought it unattractive. Well, it's true
her cheeks looked like balloons when she blew.
And who should find the flung flute in the grass
but my brother satyr, Marsyas?
Questions of cosmetics scarcely matter
to one who has the ugly mug of a satyr.
It's not for good looks that us satyrs are noted
so Marsyas blew and let his cheeks get bloated.
He took himself off to a quiet bit of wood
and girned and puffed and grunted and got good.
That peeved Apollo. He'd crossed the bounds.

Half-brutes aren't allowed to make beautiful sounds.
And can't you just hear those Muses say:
'Who gave a common satyr licence to play?'
Music 's an inner circle meant to exclude
from active participation a beast so crude.
'How can he be a virtuoso on the flute?
Look at the hooves on him. He's half a brute!'
His one and only flaw was to show that flutes
sound just as beautiful when breathed into by brutes.
It confounds their categories of high and low
when your Caliban outplays your Prospero.
If Marsyas had touched it and said 'Ooo'
the way us satyrs are supposed to do,
but he went and picked it up and blew the flute
and that was trespassing for the man/brute.

For them it would have been quite enough
to have given it one abortive puff,
a buffoonish ballooning of the brutish cheeks
producing a few and inexpert squeaks.
That would have amused them and been OK
but Marsyas, man/animal, learned to play.
To have watched him smell it, test it with his teeth
or use it like the pygmies as a penis sheath,
all allowable, all tolerated fun,
but your Apollonian goes for his gun
when it suddenly dawns on him that the swine
the pearl is cast before by one divine
knows it's a pearl, and not some novel food
and aspires beyond dumb swinetude.
When he enters the culture the 'pearl' represents
they reach for their skin-removing instruments.

They set up a contest, rigged from the start,
to determine the future of 'high' and 'low' art.
They had it all fixed that Apollo should win
and he ordered my brother to be flayed of his skin.

And the Phrygian skinner with his flaying blade
saw Apollo's pointing pinkie and obeyed.
While Marsyas suffered his terrible flaying
Apollo looked on with his 'doodah' playing.
While the Phrygian flenser slices and flays
Apollo plucks out a glib Polonaise.
And the skinners applauded Apollo's reprise
as my brother's flayed nipples flapped on to his knees.
The last thing Marsyas saw was his own skin
like a garment at his feet with no one in.

Wherever the losers and the tortured scream
the lyres will be playing the Marsyas theme.
You'll hear the lyres playing behind locked doors
where men flay their fellows for some abstract cause.
The kithara cadenza, the Muse's mezzo trill
cover the skinning and the screaming still.
Wherever in the world there is torture and pain
the powerful are playing the Marsyas refrain.
In every dark dungeon where blood has flowed
the lyre accompanies the Marsyas Ode.

Wherever the racked and the anguished cry
there's always a lyre-player standing by.
Some virtuoso of Apollo's ur-violin
plays for the skinners as they skin.

*Silenus drinks from his wineskin as if to blot out the
memory of Marsyas.*

So I don't make waves. I don't rock the boat.
I add up the pluses of being man/goat.
Unlike my poor flayed brother, Marsyas,
I've never yearned to move out of my class.
In short, I suppose, I'm not really averse
to being a satyr. I could do a lot worse.
I just have to find the best way to exist
and I've found, to be frank, I exist best pissed.

I think what's terrific about that speech is not only the anger at the division between high and low culture, which is used as a political instrument, but the fact that Apollo, who is the god of everything we understand by civilisation – music, law, light – is also the man who goes for his gun. There is almost an equation between the 'civilised' and the viciously violent.

It's a theme I've explored in other plays, that the legacy of Europe with its culture, theatre, its art, has also been a bloody, savage battlefield over the centuries. It's very hard to reconcile these two things and I'm always looking for ways to explore that dichotomy in European culture.

At its most extreme, it's the question of how a country that produced Goethe and Beethoven can also have produced Auschwitz?

Sure. I was eight years old when I first saw the pictures of Auschwitz and Belsen and Buchenwald, I was taken by the school. It haunted me so much I couldn't believe you could find joy again. It's haunted me ever since, and a lot of my work has been a way of trying to address how you relate our undoubted capacity for joy and love and friendship and culture with our ability to go on destroying each other.

This leads us on to Square Rounds, *which is a play about munitions, about bullets, and perhaps also about the astonishing irony that Alfred Nobel should endow a peace prize after making a fortune out of explosives.*

The strange thing about Alfred Nobel – and he was one of the examples that got me into the play – is that he had a choice: he didn't know whether he would become an inventor or a poet. When he was dying, he wrote a verse tragedy called *Nemesis*, about the Cenci, which Shelley had written a drama about. When you translate from an ancient play written by a poet, there is no question that it should be rendered into verse – although for many years in the theatre you got great poetic originals translated into prose – but when you're doing an original play, you have to think: Why is this thing in verse?

Nobel's one example of how explosives and poetry have something in common, and then I found out that Hiram Maxim, who invented the machine gun, had a brother, Hudson, who invented an explosive called Maximite and also wrote a book called *The Science of Poetry*, in which he analysed how poetry works. He believed if you just put it together in a scientific way, it works. His book is full of braggadoccio, and I thought this kind of energy would fill the Olivier. Then I found out that, if you remember, the deadlock in the First World War, the trench warfare, was to do with the fact that both sides had the same machine gun, the Maxim gun. Maxim could no longer sell it to the Americans, who had got rid of most of their so-called primitive peoples with the machine gun and didn't need it any more. But we needed it in our empire. Maxim came to Britain, was knighted, impressed Queen Victoria with his Maxim gun; she told her German relations, and they all bought it, so both sides had stocks of Maxim guns. The way to break that deadlock came from a man called Fritz Haber, who won the Nobel prize for bringing nitrogen out of the skies, which was like getting bread from the skies because we need nitrogen in the earth, as fertiliser. And I found out that Haber also used to run around giving verse speeches to his workers, even ordering laboratory equipment in rhyming couplets, and expecting his workers to respond in kind. Haber is also credited as being the inventor of chemical weapons in the First World War. He went from fertilising gas to asphyxiating gas.

Normally I don't read from my plays, but I've been reading a bit of *Square Rounds* recently. In *Square Rounds* all the parts were played by women. This was another promise that came out of the debates when we first did *The*

Oresteia – it was a cast of twenty-four women. The prototype of the machine gun was by a man called James Puckle, who in 1718 made a machine gun with a revolving chamber. But the ingenious part of this gun was that it had round bullets to kill Christians and square bullets to kill Muslims because they were more painful, and he advertised his machine gun in rhyming verse. The play was called *Square Rounds* because of James Puckle, who made square ammunition as being more painful. The cluster bomb which is being used illegally by the so-called 'coalition of the willing' on Baghdad and Fallujah originally used round metal ballbearings, and then some genius said if you make them square, they'll be more painful, and someone else said if you make them not of metal but of plastic, the X-rays won't be able to find them. So if I were doing it now, *Square Rounds* would come right up to date.

There was a lot of music and magic in the play – magic because it was a metaphor for chemistry. This is about James Puckle, and is a song between Sir Hiram Maxim and his brother Hudson Maxim.

Hudson Maxim
  Though the USA has led the way
  as machine-gun pioneers
  my brother knows his invention owes
  a lot to a Limey dead two hundred years . . .

Sir Hiram Maxim
  James Puckle first solved how a chamber revolved
  and achieved a sustained rate of fire.
  In 1718 he made a machine
  that killed two ways lower and higher.

Hudson Maxim
  In his own way and in his own day
  he faced the problem we face at present

67

Sir Hiram Maxim
how to use the same gun on everyone

Hudson Maxim
but distinguish the Cross

Sir Hiram Maxim
from the Crescent.

Munitionettes (*singing*)
With his Protestant zeal he fashioned the steel
that got shot from his gun in two forms.
Paradox though it sounds he fashioned *square rounds*
to kill those who scorned Christian norms.

Hudson Maxim
If it's the Cross you revere you get killed by a sphere
but if you face towards Mecca at prayer
the pain that you'll feel pierced by James Puckle's steel
is redoubled when bullets

Munitionettes
are square.

Sir Hiram Maxim
'For defending the Laws and the Protestant Cause'
he wrote of his gun with poetical flair
so a Catholic could fall by a spherical ball
but the ball for a Moslem was

Audience
square.

Hudson Maxim
In his day he'd decide how people died
according to religion or skin.
Those outside the bounds would get the square rounds
and the round rounds would slay those within.

Munitionettes

He couldn't forget the Islamic threat
and got his dual weapon to work
so that normal spheres killed Christian peers
but more painful rounds killed the Turk.

Hudson Maxim

In this day of ours with greater powers
the question of 'square rounds' is vaster
but whatever you say of death Maxim's way
there can't be many much faster.

AUDIENCE MEMBER *It wouldn't be possible for a pupil today at a state school to learn Greek and Latin as you did. How do you feel about that?*

I think it's terrible. I came from a working-class home, without books. I won a scholarship and learnt Greek. My great love affair with Greek is precisely because, as I said, I was terrified as a child by what I knew about the Second World War. I came from an inarticulate family and that gave me a passion for articulacy and learning languages. Greek gave me a model for a culture and an art, especially Greek tragedy, which addressed the worst things that we can imagine. For me it just flowed into my spirit. I think it's terrible that people won't get a chance to find that kind of magic for themselves.

AUDIENCE MEMBER *We know what you think about Eliot and Fry. Are there any poets working in the theatre that you do admire?*

Aeschylus, Sophocles, Euripides, Shakespeare, Molière, Racine, Goethe, Schiller, Lorca, Yeats, Brecht . . .

AUDIENCE MEMBER *Derek Walcott?*

Derek Walcott definitely.

AUDIENCE MEMBER *Can you tell us something about the look of a play in performance, how a production is visualised on stage?*

I was incredibly fortunate in that I worked with Jocelyn Herbert for twenty-odd years. I knew her earlier but we didn't work together till *The Oresteia* in 1981. When I started directing my own plays, even before I'd written very much, I would send thirty lines to actors like, say, Barrie Rutter or Sian Thomas, to say 'Are you interested?', to ensnare people into the play. Even before that, very early on, I would talk to Jocelyn about the look of the thing. From my work on *The Trackers of Oxyrhynchus*, I have about a dozen notebooks of ideas and images. In the first pages of them, there's a drawing of a pattern of nine crates, falling open and making a fragmentary dance floor. I went to her with this drawing and said, 'It starts like that, but I haven't written anything.' She said, 'Oh, wonderful!' Then we'd start to talk about the world of the play. For *Square Rounds* we talked about magicians, and the women were dressed like conjurors with top hats, like the women who performed dressed as men in music hall, such as Vesta Tilly. Jocelyn made the Olivier stage into this simple white floor with a black circle, like a deconstructed magician's top hat. We used silks to represent the poisonous gases that had been invented. We know that the technology of dyeing was immediately transformed, in the First World War, into making poisonous gases, so there was a logical connection, but it was also to do with the silks out of magicians' top hats. These silks became the basis of the transformation that Arturo Bracchetti, the Italian quick-change genius, did in the play, when he would catch a yellow silk, drop it and he would have a yellow costume on, then a green, then a purple. All these things I would talk to Jocelyn about. This book includes a memory of our last weekend together, when we were talking about a play

I'm writing now for the National. We were talking about it until ten minutes before she died. I hadn't got anywhere near to finishing the text, but I like to imagine the physical world as I go on.

I quoted all those poets I admire deliberately because they worked directly with actors, were always writing for actors that they knew. All the great theatre, all the great opera, came out of the relationship between the poet and the actor, the composer and the singer. We don't have that in theatre now.

AUDIENCE MEMBER *Does that make it more difficult to get a second production?*

Sure. Very difficult, because it's so tied in to the way it's created. *Trackers* actually did have a production in Australia, but it does make it difficult. It's also difficult because it's in poetic language which is hard to translate if you want a production in a non-English-speaking country where there are no poets working in the theatre.

AUDIENCE MEMBER *Would you ever consider writing in Greek?*

No. I can really only be satisfactorily creative, poetically, in my own language. I love the language and get sustenance from it but I couldn't create in it.

AUDIENCE MEMBER *How do you come up with a theme? Do you choose an actor first and play to their strengths?*

It could be a physical idea, or I think I'd like to write something for a certain actor. They tend to orbit around at the same time. I find I get quite stuck if I can't think of who's playing the part.

AUDIENCE MEMBER *How do you keep your feet on the ground in this febrile, hothouse, London atmosphere, especially with politics as they are at the moment?*

Well, I tend to come to London like a pirate, do my work and leave. I do write political poems for the newspapers, especially about our current adventures in Iraq. I write those in great rage and anger. Poetry is regarded as a spiritual endeavour. It is, but the strange thing about poetry is that it is absolutely rooted in the physical, the sensual, in the taste and feel of words. There's something in that that keeps my feet on the ground. And actually walking, with my feet on the ground, is a great way to induce and keep a sense of rhythm in your body while composing. I often compose lines and speeches while walking.

The iambic is the human step.

The human step, and the heartbeat too. Jean-Louis Barrault, the great French actor, said '*le coeur bat l'iambe*' – the heart beats iambically.

Can we end with a poem from this collection, one which relates to Jocelyn Herbert?

I was with Jocelyn the weekend she died, out at her farm in Hampshire. We had done two pieces together in Delphi – *The Trackers of Oxyrhynchus* was premiered there, before it came to the National, then in 1995, again with Barrie, we did *The Labourers of Heracles*. Jocelyn loved Greece, and one time we were sitting on a balcony in Delphi and she asked me to read poems I'd written about my parents. During this last weekend she said, 'Do you remember when you read those poems about your mother and father and their wedding rings?' and Sian, who was also there, said, 'He's written a new one.' Jocelyn said, 'Oh, read it to us.' This poem was also about rings. In Leeds there's a jeweller's called Dyson's, with a great big clock, and everybody used to meet under the clock at Dyson's. My parents, when they were courting, used to meet there. Then, when my dad proposed, they bought their engagement ring and

wedding rings from the same jeweller's. So this poem is
called 'Under the Clock'.

Under Dyson's clock in Lower Briggate
was where my courting parents used to meet.
It had a Father Time and *Tempus Fugit*
sticking out sideways into the street
above barred windows full of wedding bands,
'eternities' to be inscribed with names,
like that I felt on Dad's when we held hands,
or on Mam's crumbling finger in cremation's flames.

Today back on Briggate I stopped and saw
the red hands on the Roman XII and V
those lovers won't meet under any more,
glad stooping Father Time and I survive.
I see the scythe, the hourglass, the wings,
the Latin you'd proudly ask me to construe
and think of the padded boxes with your rings,
under the clock to keep our rendezvous.

Christopher Hampton

3 DECEMBER 2004
LYTTELTON THEATRE

Cast performing the extracts:

Horváth Rupert Wickham
Helen Emma Cunniffe

We should begin by talking about your first play, When Did You Last See My Mother?

My first play was done while I was an undergraduate at Oxford, and by some chance got a good review, not something that has happened with any regularity in my career. I got a letter from Frank Pike, the plays editor at Faber and Faber. He said 'We were very interested to read the review in *The Guardian* as we've been following your career with interest for some years, in the little magazines.' I was very puzzled by this and wrote back to him, saying, 'I don't think you can have been following my career, but it's very nice of you to say so,' and I enclosed my complete works, which were a novel and my first play. He wisely passed on the novel, but agreed to publish the play, in a new series they were bringing out, called *Introductions*. It turned out that there is another writer called Christopher Hampton, a poet, who is indeed published in the little magazines, and who occasionally writes to *The Guardian* and gets me into trouble. He wrote a letter to *The Guardian*, denouncing the wishy-washy liberalism of English playwrights and their failure to meet their responsibilities. A couple of days later I got a call from Harold Pinter. He said, 'It's Harold.' I said 'Yes.' He said, 'I haven't seen you for quite a long time.' I said, 'No, that's right.' He said, 'Perhaps we should have a drink or something.' I said, 'Is it about the letter in *The Guardian*?' He said, 'Yes, yes, yes, it is.' I said, 'Well, it's not me.' He said, 'What do you mean, it's not you?' I said, 'It's another writer called Christopher Hampton who has written to the paper on a subject he feels strongly about.'

77

He said, 'I can't believe that.' I said, 'Well, if you look in the paper, it's a Cambridge address, and I don't live in Cambridge.' There was a very long silence, and he said, 'Well, what are you going to do about it?'

Tales from Hollywood was the sixth play of yours which Faber published, and the third with some kind of historical background. What attracted you to the subject of German émigrés in Hollywood during the Second World War?

The play came about in a rather strange way. I had written a play called *Savages*, which had been done at the Royal Court, then in the West End, and then, very successfully, at the Mark Taper Forum in Los Angeles, in a very good production by Gordon Davidson, who was artistic director there. Ten years later, he called me up and said they were going to do a series of plays the next year, 1982, set in Los Angeles, because it would be the 150th anniversary of the founding of the city, and would I like to write one? I said, 'Not off the top of my head, no.' He said, 'Well, we have a list of topics . . .' And one of the topics he mentioned was German émigrés. It set off a light bulb in my head because I'd just read a book by Nigel Hamilton about how Thomas Mann and his brother Heinrich fled from Hitler and washed up in Los Angeles. Thomas was very, very successful – Nobel prizewinner, dinner with Roosevelt, all that kind of thing; Heinrich, who was principally famous at that point for having written *The Blue Angel*, had a contract with Warner Brothers and was completely bewildered and didn't know what he was going to do or how to go about it. He was there with his wife, who was slowly drinking herself to death and causing scenes wherever she went. I thought this was quite rich material. In any case, I was quite interested in the idea of people in exile, or arriving in unknown surroundings. My childhood had mostly been spent in Egypt until Britain decided to invade Suez, at which point all the British people who lived in Alexandria, where I was, were thrown out. At the age of ten, I came back to this extremely strange country to be sent to school, and have felt a sympathy with exiles and people who arrive in strange environments ever since. So the subject was very congenial to me. Also, I had had a certain amount of experience by that time with Hollywood, and it seemed to me that all these preoccupations might be usefully put together in a play. In fact, they commissioned six writers to write plays about Los Angeles, but mine was the only one they accepted. So, in the event, the Festival of Los Angeles Plays of 1982 consisted of one play in which one character after another staggered onto the stage saying, 'I can't bear another day in this shithole.'

The narrator of the play, the playwright Ödön von Horváth, wasn't in fact in Hollywood at all, was he? You gave him an extension beyond his life-span in order to perform this function for you.

My technical problem with the play was that the three writers I wanted to deal with, who were in Los Angeles during the war – i.e. Thomas Mann and his brother, and Bertolt Brecht – were hardly on speaking terms with each other. I therefore needed some kind of neutral, central figure who could be reliably sent off to drift between them, and I couldn't figure out how to do that. My first notion was to have the child of one of the émigrés as a narrator, but unfortunately Thomas Mann's six children had all grown up, and the others had none, so it wasn't going to work like that. I was in Los Angeles, starting to collate the material, and I went out to lunch with some people and was talking to them about Horváth, the first of whose plays that was ever staged in English, *Tales from the Vienna Woods*, was done here in the Olivier in 1977, and I translated it. I was talking about this, and suddenly, the penny dropping, I thought I could keep him alive. Horváth had died in a rather unusual way, in 1938. He was taking shelter from a thunderstorm on the Champs Elysées, standing under a chestnut tree which was struck by lightning. A branch fell on his head and killed him. He was actually on his way to Hollywood, having just got out of Germany. I thought I'd keep him alive for another thirteen years or so, to be the central character of this play. That served all sorts of functions because, first, he knew all these people and was friendly with them, and secondly I was able to smuggle in quite a lot of autobiographical material which had to do with my own struggles in Los Angeles.

To introduce the extract: Helen, Horváth's lover in the play, is the one fictional character in it. The play goes from the real horror of people being driven out of Nazi Germany, to the ersatz, bogus horror – a real but less serious one – of people's lives and careers being crushed by McCarthyism. I wanted a character who was an American writer, so I researched a lot of careers that had come to an end at that time and landed on a woman who'd written some television and was just starting to write screenplays. I contacted her and she agreed to meet me. Then at the last minute she wrote and said it was all too painful and she didn't want to talk to me about it. Somehow, the fact that she wrote that letter gave me what I needed as a lift-off to write the character. I met other writers who had been blacklisted, but I never met the person who, as it were, I based this character on.

Spot on Horváth.

Horváth Well, I continued to work for the Warner Brothers, hoping that none of them would notice me, and sure enough, none of them did. And, in the mean time, I found a new way, which was actually an old way, to improve my English.

Spot off. Pause. Then the lights come up on Helen Schwartz's apartment. Helen and Horváth lie entwined on the sofa. Silence.

Helen Lot of American men don't like a girl to earn eight times their salary.

Horváth This is crazy. A girlfriend who takes me out to dinner and drives me to work, you want that I complain?

Helen European men must be different.

Horváth No. I think this, er. . . . *Einstellung* . . .

Helen Attitude?

Horváth Attitude, *ja*, is also common in Europe.

Helen Then it must be just you that's different.

Horváth I'm afraid yes.

Helen Actually, this is all highly irregular. As a rule, the two-thousand-dollar-a-week writers don't talk to the thousand-dollar-a-week writers, and the thousand-dollar-a-week writers stick pretty closely together.

Horváth So you are different also.

Helen It's just I'm a nice Jewish girl. I like to have someone to look after.

Horváth Yes, I have been once married to a Jewish girl.

Helen Married?

Horváth *Ja*.

Helen You didn't tell me that.

Horváth Oh, it was just for the passport.

Helen What do you mean?

Horváth I married Maria to give her the Hungarian passport.

Helen Oh, I see. And what happened?

Horváth She used it and left. Gone with the wind.

Helen You been married many other times?

Horváth Oh, I think once is enough for anyone, don't you?

Helen I wouldn't know.

Horváth You know in the Fu Manchu movies, when he says, 'I can promise you a beautifully painful and slow, slow death'? For me this is called marriage.

Helen I see.

She disengages from him gently, gets up and crosses the room to light a cigarette. Horváth sits up.

Horváth Anyway, women have always been very kind to me.

Helen I don't know why that should be.

Horváth Me neither.

She smiles at him. Silence.

What is it with these Warner Brothers? I write all these goddam scenarios, no one ever says a word to me.

Helen You want me to explain that?

Horváth Sure.

Helen It's what I was saying before.

Horváth What?

Helen First, they really don't like to read. So if they have to read, they're going to read what cost them money.

Listen, their thirty-five-hundred-dollar-a-week writers earn more while they're taking a piss than you do all week. So whose scenarios do you think they're going to look at?

Horváth Yes, but I also am costing them money.

Helen That's peanuts, Ed. That's charity. You give a blind musician a dime, you don't expect the Goldberg Variations.

Horváth OK, but it's costing me time. Ten to five every day and the goddam bus rides, when do I have time to write? My writing?

Helen You have a lot of time. You know why? Because no one reads your scenarios. And actually it suits you that way, if the truth be known.

Horváth I suppose.

Helen So why are you complaining?

Horváth I like to be appreciated.

Helen You want them to pay you and appreciate you and shut up, right?

Horváth I think this is fair, yes. Like any artist.

They smile; then Helen looks away.

I'm sorry. I know for you this is serious business.

Helen Yes, it is.

Pause.

My folks took me to see *The Jazz Singer* in New York when I was fourteen. I thought it was terrible: God, so sentimental. But I was . . . excited by it, you know? In those days I already knew I wanted to write, but I didn't know what.

Horváth And this decided you for the movies?

Helen No. It just started me thinking. A whole new medium. Infinite possibilities. Probably the first art form since Elizabethan theatre to appeal to every age group and every class. And you can take it out to audiences anywhere in the world. Now I can't imagine writing for anything but the cinema.

Horváth I understand you theoretic.

Helen I know it hasn't happened yet, I know the business is run by greedy opportunists and yes-men and chisellers, but they can't hold out for ever. Just look at the progress that's been made in, what, not even fifteen years.

Horváth Yes, but it's too powerful for them ever to listen to ze writers . . .

Helen *The, th.*

Horváth *Ach,* zis goddam sound. I know what is his answer, St Peter, when I come and say, OK, open ze gates: 'No, no, *the, th.*'

> *She laughs, comes over and sits beside him again and takes his hand.*

Helen I liked your novels so much. I wish I could read your plays. Aren't any of them translated into English?

Horváth No, I'm sorry, I am not enough famous.

Helen What are they like, are they political, or what?

Horváth No, I think you wouldn't call them political, they don't deal about special . . . *Themen.*

Helen Issues?

Horváth No, and not from Marxist ideas, like Brecht.

Helen Who?

Horváth Bertolt Brecht, he's a writer, bit older than me.
I just write about ordinary people, how bizarre they are.
I write about life, as it regrettable is. I write about the poor,
the ignorant, about victims of society, women especially.
The Left attack always: they say easy pessimism. But they
love the people without knowing any people. I know the
people, how terrible they are, and still I like them. Also,
it turns out, my plays were not enough pessimistic.

Helen And what about the Right?

Horváth Oh, already, before ten years . . .

Helen Ten years ago.

Horváth *Ja*, I was in court for fighting in a bar with
Nazis. And when my play *Geschichten aus dem
Wienerwald*, er, *Tales from Vienna Wood*, was in Berlin
premiered, the Nazi critic said, not even an audience of
niggers would watch the play without they would protest.
I stand by my review.

Helen Well, I wish I could read German. My father has
family in Germany.

Horváth Oh? Where?

Helen Düsseldorf, I think. They're, you know, cousins,
I never met them.

Horváth And are they still in Germany?

Helen Far as I know.

*Horváth shakes his head dubiously, then looks up and
across at Helen.*

Horváth You know something, you're the best looking
playwright I ever met.

Helen That's the kind of remark I usually take exception
to.

Horváth Take exception, sorry?

Helen Don't like.

Horváth Oh. All the same, it's true.

Helen smiles at him.

Helen You want to go out this evening?

Horváth No.

Helen What do you want to do this evening?

Horváth looks at her. Silence.

Oh, so that's what you want to do this evening?

Horváth I think my English is getting better.

Helen gets up and moves away, looking back over her shoulder and smiling seductively. She leaves the room. Horváth, a slow smile spreading in anticipation, rises from the sofa and is about to follow her off, when all of a sudden the house lights snap on, startling him considerably. He moves downstage, peering into the auditorium.

That scene is actually the first of three featuring just those two characters, Scenes Seven, Fourteen and Twenty-One. Perhaps you could summarise the second of the two scenes, because it contains an ideological discussion and is also the subject of the only rewrites you did?

It was actually Gordon Davidson, who, when we did *Savages* at the Mark Taper Forum, introduced me to this unfamiliar concept of rewriting plays. I thought when they were done, they were done, but he said this was not the American way and everything was negotiable up to the last minute. So I actually rewrote *Savages* and I think improved it a bit. So when I had delivered *Tales from Hollywood* and we'd started rehearsal, Gordon said, in his usual way, 'What are we going to rewrite?' And the scene I did rewrite was the middle scene between these two, which takes place on the beach, in the face of the Pacific Ocean. She tells Horváth that she's decided to join the Communist Party, which a lot of young American writers were doing at the time. He, from his European perspective, is rather patronising about it. I rewrote the scene to tilt it in her direction, to allow her to express more fully why a young American writer would feel that way – would feel, in the middle of the war, that the thing you should do would be to join the Communist Party. I wanted to heighten the idealism of this character. That in turn heightened Horváth's argument. I think in the end we came out with a considerably better scene.

The way you rewrote it, edging towards a more direct discussion of the issues, is something you later did in The Talking Cure, *with a key scene between Jung and Freud.*

That was the last of my plays that was done here at the National, a play about the early years of Jung and Freud and psychoanalysis. Yes, the play was done earlier this year at that same theatre, the Mark Taper, and I took the opportunity to improve it a bit, I think, particularly in the treatment of the relationship between Jung and Freud. I had rather coolly dealt with this here, in terms of their purely scientific arguments. I thought that the personal arguments were somehow simmering underneath, and what I had denied the audience was a real slam-bang stand-up row. So I put that in, and it went rather well.

To set the scene for the last extract: this is their last scene together. They are in Washington and she has just been hauled up before the House Committee on Un-American Activities, to confess or deny her involvement with the Communist Party.

Helen wanders disconsolately into the circle of light.
Horváth puts his arm around her. Lights up on Helen's
apartment. Horváth leads Helen gently into the room.
She looks shattered and confused. She's formally dressed:
a suit and hat. Horváth busies himself fixing her a large
scotch and ice. She looks around as if uncertain whether
to sit down; finally she takes off her hat and throws it
down on a chair. Horváth hands her the drink and she
takes a big slug. A moment's silence, except for the clink
of the ice caused by the trembling of her hand.

Horváth All over.

Helen Yes, you said it.

She takes another swallow of scotch.

Horváth Aren't you relieved?

Helen I guess so. But all those days and nights preparing
myself and getting more and more terrified, and then to
be in and out in two minutes. As long as they're going
to destroy your career, I'd've thought the least they could
do was put a little effort into it. It's kind of insulting when
they make it so obvious how insignificant they think
you are.

Horváth It's not that. It's just they are bored with people
taking the Fifth. You heard the others: I refuse to answer
this question on the ground it might incriminate me.
They don't want to listen to this all day.

Helen Then they ought to mind their own fucking
business.

Horváth Sure. Of course.

Silence. Helen sits down. She puts her glass down.
Finally she speaks in a flat voice.

Helen I'm never going to work again.

Horváth kneels in front of her and takes her in his arms. Tears start to roll down her face, but she makes no sound.

Horváth Of course you are.

Helen No. Listen, Twentieth didn't even wait to see how it turned out. Soon as they heard I got a subpoena, they fired me.

Horváth They must have known you weren't going to name names.

Helen Jesus, how could anyone do that? How could they?

Horváth To keep the pool, the maid, the subscription to the golf club, the wife.

Helen But to inform on your friends. Jesus.

He kisses her.

Horváth I admire so much what you did. So brave.

He gets up and paces around for a moment.

What are you going to do now?

Helen I don't know.

Horváth Are you going to go back East?

Helen Why?

Pause. She looks at him.

You're all I've got now.

He looks away. Long silence.

Horváth What you did today. I . . . (*He breaks off.*)

Helen Yes?

Horváth I compare it with myself and . . .

Helen What do you mean?

Horváth Listen, there is something, all this time, I never told you.

Helen looks at him.

Helen Don't.

Horváth nods gravely.

Horváth Yes, I must. (*He takes a deep breath.*) In 1934 I joined the German Writers' Union.

Helen Well, I don't see what . . . (*She breaks off: her expression changes.*) In 1934?

Horváth That's right, I should say the Nazi Writers' Union.

Helen I . . . don't understand. Why?

Horváth If you wanted to get work or to be published, you had to join.

Helen Oh, I see.

Horváth No, because it was not only this. I had to swear an oath that not even one of my grandparents was Jewish. I had to be certified . . . politically unobjectionable.

Helen You don't have to tell me all this.

Horváth No, I must get this right, it was more than this. I had to find witnesses, what you call them, references, to say I was politically reliable. One I asked was this old cretin professor who had written a book, *Adolf Hitler: Progress through Will-Power.* He signed. He said I was . . . most suitable.

Silence.

So, my boot also was on your people's faces.

Long silence.

Only thing I can say in my defence, I never paid the dues.

Neither of them smiles.

I was in two and a half years before they threw me out, and in all that time, nothing I wrote was worth shit.

Helen I don't understand how you could want to do that.

Horváth Did you read *Death in Venice*?

Helen Yes, of course.

Horváth It was a little like this, I could not leave the plague-infested city. But it was not beauty and innocence which kept me . . . enthralled, it was the grotesque, the triumph of stupidity, the ugliness.

Silence.

But no, there are no excuses.

Pause.

I should have told you before.

Helen shakes her head.

Years, since years this has been a stone in my heart.

Helen gets up and moves uncertainly around the room for a moment. Then she goes over, sits next to Horváth and takes hold of his arm.

Helen It won't make any difference.

Horváth It will.

She shakes her head again and kisses him. He holds her close for a moment.

Yes it will.

*Slowly he detaches himself from her and moves
downstage as the lights fade on Helen.*

It did. A month later she left for New York; but she'd
already travelled further away from me than the width of
a continent.

In Hampton on Hampton, *you describe* Tales from Hollywood *as a confrontation between autobiography and
history, and you mentioned autobiography earlier on.
What elements of autobiography are there in* Tales from
Hollywood?

Well, specifically, the first time I ever went to Los Angeles
was to discuss a film being made from an early play of
mine called *Total Eclipse*. In characteristic fashion, the
meeting lasted about twenty minutes, and then the producer said he had to go and play tennis with somebody,
and did I want to take a swim in his pool? I was a little bit
taken aback, but he said there were swimming costumes in
the pool house, and 'Goodbye, great to meet you.' So I had
a swim, up and down, in a rather self-conscious way, and
swam into the marble staircase that led down into the pool
and cut my head open. I fortunately managed to get out of
the pool and the next I knew was that I was lying beside
the pool, and the guy's chauffeur was standing above me,
looking down at me as if I was just taking a nap, and saying, 'Where d'you wanna go?' I said, 'The Continental Hyatt
House Hotel on Sunset.' He said, 'Oh shit! That's miles
away.' Anyway, I got dressed and left, and came back to
England and of course never heard another word about
Total Eclipse. I should have taken this as a warning, or a
sign about what it was going to be like dealing with
Hollywood, but I didn't. I persisted.

So I put this incident into the play, only Horváth doesn't
manage to get out of the pool. The other thing I put in was

that when I was very young I was hired to write a screenplay based on *Edward II* by Marlowe, in which Ian McKellen had just had a great success on stage. I wrote the screenplay in two weeks, as instructed. It was that period at the end of the sixties when American producers were rushing over here, for some reason or other, and making films. But when I went to meet this chap in his rented apartment in Eaton Square, as I came into the room, he left it, returned, and hurled the script across the room at me. He said, 'What's that?' I picked it up and said, 'It's my script.' He said, 'You wouldn't get it on fucking television.' At this point the director arrived, and it turned out that there were two things that really shocked the producer. One was that the script was in verse. We tried to explain to him that the play was in verse. The other thing was that the king of England was a faggot, which was totally unacceptable. He kept saying, 'I've got people coming in from the coast!' Eventually the director, a nice man called Douglas Hickox, no longer with us, said, 'I don't think you're being fair to Christopher,' at which point he said, 'You shut up, you're fired as well.' So Douglas and I went out to dinner. The incident found its way, pretty much unchanged, into *Tales from Hollywood*.

The play was revived at the Donmar in 2001. How do you think that production compared to previous productions at the National and the Mark Taper, and did you feel the play had survived the test of time?

It's very, very nice when people revive your plays, I must say. The first production, at the Mark Taper Forum, was very badly received. The *Los Angeles Times*, the only really important paper there, absolutely detested it, so I was a bit discouraged after that production, although I'd thought we'd done a lot of good work. The production was not entirely successful, but I thought it a very good account of the play. When I got back to England, I submitted the play to the National and was really very pleased when they accepted it immediately and scheduled it at the Olivier. Then we were very lucky with the casting. Michael Gambon was absolutely, for me, unforgettable in the part, on this vast sky-blue stage that Alison Chitty had painted. It was shortly after *Galileo*, and he was an actor who hadn't made as much of a mark as he has now. He was dazzling in the part, and the whole experience was very happy. So, twenty years pass, and they wanted to do it again at the Donmar. I was a little concerned about reducing the scale of it, but in many ways it worked even better in an intimate setting, I was pleased to find, and John Crowley did an excellent production. I hadn't written a play for a while and I was literally so encouraged by the experience of seeing it again at the Donmar that I went off immediately and wrote *The Talking Cure* – it stimulated me to write another play, so it was a very fruitful revival for me.

AUDIENCE MEMBER *I'd like to know what you're working on now?*

Two plays! One is for the National Theatre and is based on a book that came out a couple of years ago called *White Mughals*. It's set in India around 1800 and is about the machinations of the East India Company and a romance that took place between the Resident of Hyderabad and a Muslim princess, who got married at that time, and how their love was used politically by both the Indians and the British, who were jostling for control of various parts of India. It's a fascinating book by a man called William Dalrymple. I've just been in India for the first time, starting to do the research. That's a long-term project which will take a while, as there's so much research to do. In the meantime, I'm just finishing an adaptation of a book called *Embers,* by an extraordinary Hungarian writer called Sándor Márai who died in 1989 in San Diego. He lived through forty or fifty years of total obscurity, after having been very famous in his thirties, in Hungary before the war. He shot himself and left a suicide note saying that none of his plays or novels were to be published in Hungary until such time as there was a democratic election, verified by foreign observers, which happened a couple of months later. So they began to republish his work in Hungary and it slowly seeped out. This book *Embers* had a great success a couple of years ago, and I was very haunted by it. To my absolute amazement, this week, I got hold of an obscure book that he wrote in the sixties in America about Hungary during the war, and for the first time saw a photograph of him on its back. He looks *exactly* like Horváth, like Horváth's plumper brother. I don't know what it is with Hungarians, but they obviously speak to some corner of my psyche.

AUDIENCE MEMBER *As a successful playwright, you clearly have no problem in acquiring the rights for adaptations, either in terms of your reputation or, presumably, the money. Would you have anything to say about acquiring rights to someone who's less well known?*

I think the only way you can acquire rights is to strike up some kind of relationship with the author. It isn't always easy. I rather foolishly wrote a screenplay based on *The Moon and Sixpence* by Somerset Maugham without securing the rights, and this has been a field day for my learned friends. Yesterday morning at seven o'clock the producer had a meeting with some French people to try and untangle this appalling mess. I've spoken to Maugham's grandson, who is very keen for the film to go ahead, but this particular book is embroiled in all kinds of complex arrangements, so we may never manage to disentangle it. But generally what you do is to approach the publishers and then try to persuade the writer that he should let you do it. And unless it's something that's a big best-seller, I don't think large amounts of money are necessary. Most writers are absolutely delighted if you ask to adapt their books, and the way it works, even with moderately successful writers, is that the options are usually pretty modest.

AUDIENCE MEMBER *Thinking about* Dangerous Liaisons, *having written it as a play, how did it feel to adapt it into a film?*

I had chosen, I think wisely as it turned out, Stephen Frears to direct the film, and he's a man who can't bear the theatre, so he was very anxious to make it as different as possible from the play as I could manage. I was also keen to do that, because I think the problem with a lot of plays that are adapted for films is that they somehow smell of the theatre, they don't re-forge an identity of their own. This takes me to a theory I've always had, which is that films are more like novels than they are like plays. The freedoms and constraints are the same, but are completely different from the constraints you have in the theatre. The fact is that the movie *Dangerous Liaisons* is much closer to the original novel than the play was, and what I found myself doing, in short, was to go back to the novel and start again, to rethink it in terms of images. Stephen would get extremely nervous if there was a scene which lasted more than a page. He'd ask, 'What's everyone going to *do*, while all this is going on?' Towards the end of the film there are scenes which are pretty much identical to scenes in the play, but they had to be negotiated line by line.

AUDIENCE MEMBER *When you're writing a play, do you have in your mind the scale of the space you're writing for, and does that impinge on how you tell the story?*

I think sometimes you do start off with that, but it doesn't always stick. For example, in my mind this *White Mughals* adaptation is something that will probably sit in the Olivier. On the other hand *Liaisons* was written for the Barbican, and I think when they received it at the RSC they were rather disappointed, and didn't think there was much potential in it. Slowly it got negotiated down from the Barbican to The Other Place, which at that stage was a tin shed in a car park. I was not best pleased about this, particularly when I had the first design meeting with Bob Crowley and he said that they had a permanent set. I'd imagined there would be lots of lavish chateau sets. I said, 'Why does it have to be a permanent set?' He said, 'Well, the thing about The Other Place is that there is no wing space. If you take the sofa out and it's raining, when it comes back in again, it's wet.' So I said, 'Fair enough.' But it turned out to be the best thing that could possibly happen to the play, because it then opened in a 150-seat theatre and worked its effect by the powerful feeling audiences had of being in the same room with these people, everything taking place in a very conversational tone, not declaimed from a big stage. Part of the initial impact of the play had to do with this lucky break. I subsequently found out that the reason the RSC was so nervous about it was that they had mounted an adaptation of *Les Liaisons Dangereuses* in the sixties, under the title *The Art of Love*, and absolutely no one had come to see it at all. As so often in the theatre, the more limitation you have, the more fruitful it can be. Since then, my feeling has always been, let's open it in as small a space as possible, because it tends to connect with an audience in a much more visceral way than in a big public space. You think about these things when you're writing, of course, but what you think may not have any relevance to the final result.

AUDIENCE MEMBER *Which has been your happiest experience of Hollywood, and didn't you work with David Lean once?*

Dangerous Liaisons is I suppose a Hollywood picture, but not really. It was a very happy experience because nobody came from Warner Brothers as it was only $14,000,000, so we were able to make exactly the film we wanted to make, and they quite liked it when they saw it. I worked for a year with David Lean, at the end of his life, on an adaptation of Conrad's *Nostromo*. It was a very difficult adaptation and I guess some might say he was not a very easy man, but I liked him very much and feel I learned an enormous amount from him. Unfortunately he died about six weeks before shooting began, and I had long gone. I worked for him for a year and resigned in order to do the *Liaisons* script, because he was not a person you worked for part-time. But I did work with him for a year and it was a most educational experience. I think I learned more about writing films – which never came as naturally to me as writing for the theatre – out of the year working with him, than I did at any other point in my life. So I'm very grateful to him, I was very fond of him, and I'm sorry the film never got made.

Frank McGuinness

6 DECEMBER 2004
LYTTELTON THEATRE

Cast performing the extract:

Rima Sorcha Cusack
Alec Nigel Cooke

It almost goes without saying that Frank McGuinness is one of Ireland's foremost playwrights. He's the author of a dozen original plays and numerous translations, the most recent of which was his acclaimed version of Euripides' Hecuba *at the Donmar. The best known of his plays include 1985's* Observe the Sons of Ulster Marching Towards the Somme, *a piece that imagined the wartime experience of a group of Ulster Protestant volunteers and was extraordinary not least because McGuinness himself was raised Republican Catholic. A resumé of his CV must also mention* Someone Who'll Watch Over Me, *his hostage drama of 1992, inspired by the experiences of Brian Keenan, John McCarthy and Terry Waite, and, the main subject of this conversation,* Dolly West's Kitchen, *which premiered at the Abbey Theatre, Dublin, in a production directed by Patrick Mason that transferred to the Old Vic in 2000. There it attracted glowing notices – the* Daily Telegraph *pronounced it 'McGuinness' finest work to date', while* The Spectator *argued, 'No play has ever looked into Ireland's past and found there its future with the mix of wit and wisdom, death and despair, life and love that characterises every line, every corner and every moment of* Dolly West's Kitchen.'*

We're going to hear an extract in a moment which will I think explain what all the fuss was about, combining as it does a few of the play's characteristically quick-witted lines with some of its most politically provocative remarks. What you need to know in outline, if you haven't seen the play or read it before, is that this is a play set during the Second World War in Buncrana, County Donegal, and more specifically in the kitchen of the West family. The Wests are an entertainingly odd bunch. There's outspoken, sixty-something matriarch Rima, who describes herself as 'a bad bitch that says what she likes'. Rima's two daughters are the unhappily single Dolly and unhappily married Esther, and son Justin, a repressed young military nationalist with an entrenched hatred of the British. Passions are stirred by the arrival onto the scene of an Englishman, Dolly's old flame Alec, and two handsome young American GIs, who are stationed with him over the border in Northern Ireland. You'd expect major emotional upheavals to follow hard upon this friendly allied incursion into the neutral Irish free state, and sure enough you get them, but not quite in the way you initially anticipate. Crucially, Justin's furious enmity is seen to conceal the love that dare not speak its name.

Before we go into the extract, I just wanted to ask Frank to explain a little more about the scene we're to hear.

It's at a certain stage in the mother Rima's life, when she knows that each of her three children, Dolly, Esther and Justin, is going through a sexual crisis, and that something needs to be done soon so that they will resolve their unhappiness and make something of their lives. In this particular scene, Rima is applying her formidable pressure on Alec to marry Dolly, to make an honest woman of her, as she says. What has preceded this is that Alec has made an advance on the young maid, Anna, who's only in her teens.

Rima There's an awful smell of spilt milk. Have you been crying, Alec? Running after young ones – did you think she would takes years off you? Leave her to the Yanks. Make an honest woman of Dolly.

Alec She wouldn't take me.

Rima You haven't asked her

Alec I know her answer.

Rima Isn't she wise, then? Imagine being stuck with you making a pass after skirt that won't rise for you?

Alec Is that what happened to you and your husband?

Rima Who told you that – Dolly?

Alec I'm sorry – no – I shouldn't have –

Rima It was Ned then.

He nods his head.

That poor man's been dreading Esther will leave him since the day – hour they married.

Alec Will she?

Rima If she does she'll come back. Her father did. And he gave me a final gift – his son. That's why Justin is ten years younger than Dolly. He was always good at the giving – my man. Not just to me, but to all his fancy women. Still, there was enough to spare. I was left the house and a fair share of money. We were well off. Dolly could get to Trinity College –

Alec Where Catholics aren't supposed to go.

Rima Which is why she went. The same one was never Gospel greedy.

Alec Did he live to see his son Justin born?

Rima Just about. Sad that.

Alec Did Justin mind not having his father?

Rima Ask if I missed his father?

Alec Did you?

Rima I did, Alec.

Alec And you never –

Rima Strayed? No. When you give your heart and it's broken, you don't give it again. Well, I didn't anyway.

Alec Maybe I should make a pass at you, Rima?

Rima If I found a man's hand up my skirt now, I wouldn't know what he was looking for. Why don't you marry?

Alec My father – my mother –

Rima So?

Alec I didn't want to inflict the same unhappiness. Her crying like a lost child sitting on the bed beside me. Him walking the floor of their bedroom trying to make sense of what they'd done to each other. When she died, he kept on walking the floor – they should have separated long before they started living for the sole reason of hating each other. They kept on together – I'll never know why.

Rima We never know. I'll tell you a true story happened in this town. Two old women sitting drinking in a pub. In walked a beautiful young girl carrying a bunch of roses and wearing what looked like a brown dish cloth on her head. One old one – we'll call her Mary – she says, I swear to Christ that's the little flower, St Therese of Lisieux. The other one says, what would St Therese of Lisieux be doing in a pub in Buncrana? I swear it's her, Mary says. There's only way to find out, ask her. So Mary goes over and says to the young one with the dish cloth, excuse me, myself and my friend was wondering if you are the little flower, St Therese of Lisieux? The young one looks up from under the dish cloth and says, would you ever fuck off? Mary goes back and the friend says, is it her? Is it St Therese of Lisieux? Mary says, I asked her if

she was the little flower and she told me to fuck off.
That's a pity, says the friend, now we'll never know.

Alec And that happened in this town?

Rima Well, it didn't happen in Moville.

Alec Poor Moville.

Rima Moville my bollocks.

Alec You don't have bollocks, Rima.

Rima You haven't put your hand up my skirt – caught
you there.

Alec You're an honest woman, Rima.

Rima I'm a bad bitch that says what she likes. Give me
an honest answer to this, Alec. How's the war going to
shape?

Alec It's touch and go.

Rima Still? The Germans?

Alec Mad.

Rima The English?

Alec Angry.

Rima The Yanks?

Alec Savage.

Rima Are they savage enough?

Alec Yes, they are.

　　Silence.

Rima And the Jews?

　　Silence.

Is it as bad –?

Alec It's worse, I think. We don't know –

Rima We do.

Silence.

If any country should have opened the door to any people facing what they are facing – Ireland –

Alec It might not be as bad –

Rima We did nothing to save them.

Alec Ireland's a neutral country.

Rima Do you believe that?

Alec No.

Rima Neither do I.

I just want to repeat the last of the lines we just heard: 'Ireland's a neutral country.' 'Do you believe that?' 'No.' 'Neither do I.' That's an extraordinary series of lines, so small and yet asking such a huge question. Was Irish neutrality, the myth or the fact of it, the trigger for this play? Was that the question uppermost in your mind when you sat down to write it?

I never think there's just one trigger for a play, it's a whole variety of things. But certainly I'm intrigued by the subject of neutrality and I'm torn by the subject. I think you've got to remember that an awful lot of Irish men and Irish women fought against Hitler in the Second World War; they did join the British army and they fought with the Americans and Canadians. I'm not ashamed of that, actually. De Valera, who was the prime minister, the Taoiseach, at the time was in a terrible position. He had just taken the ports back, it was a very poor country, and if he had allied himself with the British there would have been serious

opposition to it. If he had shown himself to be too
favourable to Churchill, it wouldn't have gone down too
well. However, that said, I think the dilemma of the Second
World War, the fight against Fascism, was the defining
moment of European history, and that those who did fight
did the right thing. I do believe we should have been
involved; that's what my heart says, and my head says it as
well. I firmly don't believe that we were neutral. I think as
far as it was possible we did a reasonable, small amount to
assist the Allies. I know that much was made of the fact
that de Valera went to the German Embassy to sign a book
of condolence on Hitler's death, and I feel that was a *dis-
graceful* act; there are ways of not doing that, you know.
But that said, it was a very hard time and a very hard decision to make. I'm actually quite proud of Ireland's neutrality and the fact that most of our military history has
been as peacekeepers with the United Nations. My own
family, both on my father's and my mother's side, has very
close contacts with Irish soldiers – uncles, cousins who
served, and I'm quite proud of that fact. The Second World
War was a truly terrible time against a terrible enemy and
if by any chance Germany *had* invaded, I don't think
Hitler would have been too much in love with the Irish. He
planned to transport most of us to mines in Poland; the
Celts were not high on his list of acceptable Aryans.

*Were you conscious of this being a difficult issue to explore
in such a public forum, when the play was staged originally in Ireland? Was it a debating point for people? Did
they want to have some means of channelling their feelings
about this period?*

No, I think it's not that raw a wound, neutrality in Ireland.
It's just taken as a given that militarily we are neutral, or
say we are. We allow US planes to be refuelled in Shannon –
that's how neutral we are in that particular conflict. That
makes a nonsense of neutrality. The notorious leader

Charles Haughey had a wicked description: 'Irish solutions for Irish problems.' Part of that solution is forgetfulness, or a willingness to live with contradiction, and I think that was part and parcel of the response to the play. It wasn't really seen as that big an attack on neutrality. I was sorry about that, actually, that it didn't provoke more.

Was it more provocative in the sense that Justin, the most fearful and bigoted character initially, who was absolutely opposed to even breathing the same air as the British, comes across in the later stages of the play as the one who is infatuated with the overtly homosexual American GI? Did that cause any . . . ?

Yeah, that caused bother. An Irish soldier being homosexual did raise eyebrows. In the first act of the play, when Marco, the gay GI, and Justin are on the beach, slowly but surely you become aware that there is something happening between these two. One night during this scene, when Marco takes a cigarette and kisses Justin's hand, a woman in the audience cried out, 'Oh Jesus, that's what's wrong with him!' She was honest enough to shout it out, but it really wasn't too approved of that we would have the suggestion, even, that Justin was gay and put that on stage in the National Theatre of Ireland, even in the year of 1999.

Did it nearly cause a riot?

Not quite a riot, sure they're too clever now for riots, they don't do that any more; they write to the *Irish Times*.

Critics over here didn't get into a stew about it, but they did wonder how wilfully anachronistic you were being because, as we heard then, some of the language is extremely colourful, and certainly the frankness with which Marco shares his feelings doesn't strike a chord with one's perception of the forties as being quite an illiberal, repressed time.

I did my research very carefully on gays in the American army, and on gay history through the twentieth century, particularly the gay history of New York. And I tell you, in the 1940s, when America went to war, there was no 'don't ask, don't tell' policy. They took you on if you could handle a gun, there was no problem about it. If you look at these military histories written from the gay point of view, of which there are quite a few now, there was no shortage of gay men in the armed forces. I knew of one particular wonderful individual – he's dead now. He spent his war in Asia, but his contribution was that he and four other drag queens went from those little bolt-holes that they had down there to perform in shows, in the middle of battle. They were in there, in full gear, doing their numbers, and let's just say repressed this guy wasn't. They were incredibly popular and there was no question of drumming them out, there was no disguise about it. Of course there were periodic purges and panics, and the punishment for being caught was pretty severe, but they were few and far between. There was no shortage of gay men in the army and quite a few of them were pretty open about it as well.

I wanted to ask you to tie it into your own life experience. Clearly the play is set some ten years or so before you were born, but in very much the same place. Were you consciously rooting it in that particular spot for autobiographical reasons?

I was born in 1953 and it was only when I started to research this play that I realised – the war finished *eight years* before I was born. To me, the Second World War when I was a kid was like the Roman Empire, it was that far away. And it shocked me – I was in my mid-forties and wrote the play and it hit me – I thought, 'Oh my God, I am the product of the Second World War.' Eight years before, that's like 1996 from now. Buncrana was in an extraordinary position during the Second World War because it was one of these ports that had been handed back to the Irish. It's a natural fjord, it's very deep, so they could have taken major ships in. They were living in dread that the British might take back the ports and Buncrana would have been one of the first to be taken back. The other thing was that there was this influx of American soldiers, especially, from Derry. Some people had a very good war, my mother being one of them; she certainly remembered these gods arriving – these men who were tanned and who had teeth! An extra-ordinary change came over the sexual morality of that town for that period. There was an immense amount of money being made, because Ireland wasn't suffering from the rationing the way they were here in England. People were coming over to eat and drink and do what they wanted. I'm not saying Buncrana girls of my mother's generation were 'loose' but they were probably looser than the generation that came after – my generation – and the one that came before them. So here was all this stuff on my doorstep, waiting to be explored. I don't look gift horses in the mouth, so that was one of the major reasons for writ-ing the play, because of the intimate, detailed access I had to a very special time and its place in the town's history.

You implied that Rima was your mother. Was she very much based on your mother?

My mother died while I was plotting the play and it then became very much her play and her voice. Everything that Rima says in the play, the most outrageous things that Rima says, my mother said. She worked in a shirt factory, she left school when she was fourteen, she was an incred-ibly clever woman, very funny, very quick. She'd zap the bastards down, she didn't give a shit for anybody. She was politically very astute, didn't buy extremism from any quarter, not her scene. In the course of the play, at the end of the scene you heard, Rima dies. It's about halfway through the second half, and whatever the controversy about neutrality or gays in the army, *killing the Irish mother half way through the second half of the play . . .!* There were audiences I thought were going to kill me. Killing the Irish mother – they don't like it. I'd try to explain that the whole play was about surviving the death of your mother, that's absolutely where it stems from. But there was just horror and shock when they discover Rima is dead and not play-acting as she had done in the first half. My mother would have loved this – in 1996 I was refused communion at my mother's funeral as the demon queer, can you believe that? – but in the play she is given a funeral with Irish soldiers, British soldiers and American soldiers carrying her coffin, and Monteverdi playing. She would have loved that. I couldn't give it to her in life but I gave it to her in the play.

It sounds as if the party was over by the time you came along. The liberation the Americans had brought had faded into the background. You've described Buncrana as no-man's-land, close enough to the border to be continually intrigued by what lay beyond it. In a way that has a peculiar figurative resonance for your own self, crossing at some point the border between accepted Catholic morality and repression, and homosexual liberation. Do you see them as connnected in some way?

Ah yes, definitely. I certainly see that where I come from has a crucial bearing on my own imagination and on what I'm attracted to write about, no question of that. I'm very interested in division, disguise, instability, not merely because of my own awareness of my homosexuality. You're right to say the party was over, there was a lot less money around in the fifties. Ireland got a little bit prosperous in the sixties but I remember seeing my uncle's wage packet in the late sixties: it was £8 a week, and they'd be working in the shirt factory for even less. So most people were still at subsistence level or just above – and then, the miracle.

The EEC, the Common Market. I cannot tell you how that transformed Ireland. But the fifties and sixties were really hard times. What was happening was the development of the war in the north. That had been simmering, of course, from the foundation of the Northern Irish state. In the sixties especially there were signs that something was going to erupt, and in 1969, absolute eruption, but 1966 was the beginning. I was about thirteen in 1966, going through puberty when this was all just about to happen, and we were so close to the epicentre, which for a long time was Derry. Ironically enough, I was on holiday in Dublin when it did explode. I have no doubt about it that that sense of borders and crossing and going into unknown territory had a crucial bearing on my writing.

It sounds as though it would have been tough growing up there even if you just wanted to be a playwright. You started writing at thirty, didn't you?

I'd written poems and short stories, and then the big substantial thing when I was twenty-nine or thirty: I wrote *The Factory Girls*. Unwittingly I had been serving a bit of an apprenticeship till then in that I had acted, as a postgraduate student, and I had directed student productions when I was teaching in my first job at the University of Ulster at Coleraine, so all that was getting experience without really knowing it. But yes, growing up in Buncrana in the sixties when you're kind of aware that something was not quite right, though of *course* it's all right to be gay . . . Anyway, I learnt how to fight because if I hadn't I would have been killed. I think everybody that grew up in that town in the sixties . . . put it like this, there wasn't much that could scare them, you know? It wasn't a pretty place, it was a tough, tough town. All the tougher for the fact that it was a town whose economy depended on female labour, which meant that the men were really tough. I left in 1971, and I was kind of glad to leave it. It is my home and it always will be my home and I was shaped by it very decisively, but I was glad to leave it. My parents never went beyond primary school education, but I was the first generation to get free secondary school education and free university education, and I became a university lecturer in 1977. My mother and father absolutely accepted that as a good job but they never really caught on to the theatre. I think they thought this nonsense wasn't going to last, it was so far away from their own experience. There was no theatre in Buncrana; we had pantomimes very occasionally, but theatre was so way out of their understanding or their interest, even. They were glad about it, but to them it was a side career to the main one, which was teaching.

Not even publication by Faber and Faber guaranteed their recognition of your success?

Oh, they were very proud to have all the books on show. But my joy about being with Faber and Faber was two-fold: T. S. Eliot and W. H. Auden – to me that was Faber. When Frank Pike, who was drama editor at the time, said he wanted to publish *Observe the Sons of Ulster*, it was one of the happiest days of my life. I was going to be a Faber author! I could almost have changed my name to Frank Austen so that it would be next to Auden on the list. It just was a very big deal for me that Faber would be my publishers.

And they've published not just your original plays but also your translated works, of which the top seller is A Doll's House.

Janet McTeer, God love her, has been a great little money-spinner for me. I had my version and Janet had hers – she kept improvising.

Hecuba *has just been on at the Donmar and* Electra *prior to that. And* Mutabilitie, *one of your most important, epic plays, was done here at the National five or six years ago. But we don't see all of them. We've just caught up with* Gates of Gold *at the Finborough. Do you feel there's a slight divide, are there certain plays of yours that you wish had been seen in London but haven't?*

Oh yeah. *Gates of Gold* is an example of that. When it was done in Dublin it did OK business, got OK reviews, had a very good cast of English and Irish, but there was no interest here at all till this letter arrived from the Finborough. Gavin McAlinden was absolutely passionate to do the play and that to me is key. If you're that hungry to do it, you're going to do something with it. The director is twenty-four or twenty-five and I'd thought only somebody in their fifties would want to do a play like that.

I remember you were saying that when Dolly West's Kitchen *was very well received here, you were pleased but slightly suspicious. You didn't want it to be pigeonholed as a rural kitchen Irish drama. The plays you write are so varied but people want to be able to pigeonhole you.*

Well, they do. It's a tendency of bad critical writing if that's what they want from you, and it's also bad playwriting if you let them do that. When I'm writing a play, I want to shock myself with where I'm going to go or what I'm going to do. I never know. There were very good reviews for *Dolly West's Kitchen*. The reviews for *Mutabilitie* were not terribly good. The wise Michael Gambon said, 'Don't read them. If they're good they flatter you and if they're bad they make you cry; and if you read the good ones and believe them, you've got to read the bad ones as well.'

AUDIENCE MEMBER *How do you start translating from another language? Do you start from scratch, and do you speak all those languages?*

I did Old Norse for four years when I was a student. I remember my mother asking what I was doing, and I told her English, Anglo-Saxon and Old Norse. 'What's that?' And I told her it was the language of the sagas and the basis of the Scandinavian languages. And she replied, 'Oh that's great, son, you'll never be out of a job with that skill.' To my dying day it will be my regret that the night *Doll's House* won the Tony award for best revival, I couldn't ring her and say, 'Jesus, Ma, you were right, I have not been out of a job, actually.' When I do a version I absolutely have to be burning mad committed to the play. I've been carrying a flame for *Hecuba*, as Thelma Holt will tell you, for over four years. I have to have an obsession for the play if I'm going to do it, but I have to go in there and tackle it from scratch. I'm very lucky with the people who do my literal translations because they give me what I want, which is something completely unintelligible, that's what I'm looking for. They will give me that raw, rough stuff. For *Hecuba* it was my friend Fionnuala Murphy, who is an actress but a classical scholar as well. If you saw what she gave me and what I was doing with it for the first four or five pages – it was this monstrous thing. I was so ready to give it up, but I had to keep going with it until I had something that was speakable.

What I want to do is to work through that passion, that obsession, incorporate it into my own stamina and my own writing skills, and then it will come out in a new play. I do these versions for absolutely selfish reasons – because I want to know how that play works, in so far as I'm able to understand it. It's no good my going to other translations. I guarantee for every play I've done there are much more scholarly texts than anything I can do. But my teaching purposes and my writing purposes will be combined in this slog to get this play into my head and to know it. So what I require is somebody with a brilliant knowledge of the original language, who will be willing to do a demolition job for me and then let me build, in my flawed way, what I can with it. I'm always aware that versions like mine have a short life. They will last ten, fifteen years, then someone else will come along and do it in another way. It's an exercise in humiliation as well, actually, when you see what Ibsen can do with a play like *A Doll's House*.

AUDIENCE MEMBER *I was asked recently to read* Someone Who'll Watch Over Me *by someone who's thinking of staging it, and I'm wondering if you see a subtle difference now with the changes in the political arena?*

Oh God, yes, I read it again recently for the first time in ten years. I think the American character would have a different interpretation because of what's happened. But what I would very much like the play to explore this time is how important for each of these men the relationship with their father is. In a way that's what I think is at the very heart of the play – men's relationships with their fathers and with each other, which are deep. I don't want to say they're not sexual because that gives the wrong target. I will never forget something that made me angry, someone who read the play in manuscript form and said, 'Oh God, I'm so relieved, there are no queers in this one.' I was ready to kill him – it was a very well-known director and he meant we had a chance of making some money this time. But that's so not what the play is about. I would love to go back and work on it again and see what happens in terms of the present climate. I don't know, is the answer. Once I finish a play I finish it. It's done. But I think it's more the politics of men than the politics of the Middle East.

AUDIENCE MEMBER *When you're writing something with characters from different places and generations, how much do you focus on the language? And do you find it difficult?*

No, actually. For me the three dominant forms of English are English-English, Irish-English and American-English, and I love working with them. I did it in *Someone Who'll*

Watch Over Me and I did it in *Dolly West's Kitchen*. I love writing American-English because I love American actors, I love working with them, I love their daring. I do very consciously enjoy that process of using the different dialects.

AUDIENCE MEMBER *How do you fit your writing in with your teaching?*

When I started writing, I didn't have a job. The Irish economy was in the pits at that time, the early eighties. We were in the EEC but the oil prices had really hit us badly. Only certain sections of the population were doing well out of the EEC, I had no job and I really wanted to write a novel or a play before I was thirty. Then I did get a job in 1983, a part-time job that turned into a full-time job. The fact is that I really really enjoy teaching, and I didn't earn that much money from writing. When *Observe the Sons of Ulster* was done here at Hampstead, I made less than two grand from it, and not much more in Dublin, so I couldn't afford to write full-time, still cannot really, if truth be told. But I'm fifty-one now and I'm beginning to find it hard to do the two. They're very good to me in the college I work at, my official title is Lecturer in English, but they look on the writing as my research. I concentrate my intense teaching into three or four months from January through the first semester. This year I've got study leave so I've just come out of a pretty hectic teaching time, but I am not overworked, they're incredibly good to me. I really like the people I work with, as well, which is a big advantage, and I like my students. I'm a mean mother-fucker, so if they get through a course with me, they've been through it, you know, but I enjoy working with them a lot.

You've got a play coming up at the RSC. Do you want to talk about that?

Yes, in September at the Swan. It's called *Speaking Like Magpies* and it's about the various figures on the fringes of the Gunpowder Plot. They asked me to do it, and I didn't know anything about the Gunpowder Plot until I went and researched it. The actual plotters themselves I didn't find particularly fascinating, but people like King James and Robert Cecil and Henry Garnet, they intrigued me an awful lot. The whole idea of equivocation spurred the play into what I'm doing. I told Dominic Cooke, if you want a play with twelve guys in big hats whispering behind their hands, go elsewhere. At the heart of the play there's a Jacobean masque and that's where the details of the Gunpowder Plot come through. *Mutabilitie* was spoken of as 'a travesty of English and Irish history' – so it's another travesty.

We shall eagerly await your next travesty. Thank you very much.

The Playwrights

DAVID HARE was born in Sussex in 1947. Thirteen of his plays have been produced at Britain's National Theatre. A trilogy about the Church, the Law and the Labour Party – *Racing Demon*, *Murmuring Judges* and *The Absence of War* – was presented in repertory at the Olivier Theatre in 1993. Two of his plays, *The Permanent Way* and *Stuff Happens*, premiered at the National in 2004. Nine of his best-known plays, including *Plenty*, *The Secret Rapture*, *Skylight*, *The Blue Room*, *Amy's View*, *The Judas Kiss* and *Via Dolorosa* – in which he performed – have also been presented on Broadway.

TOM STOPPARD's work includes *Enter a Free Man*, *Rosencrantz and Guildenstern Are Dead*, *The Real Inspector Hound*, *Jumpers*, *Travesties*, *Night and Day*, *Every Good Boy Deserves Favour* (with André Previn), *After Magritte*, *Dirty Linen*, *The Real Thing*, *Hapgood*, *Arcadia*, *Indian Ink*, *The Invention of Love* and the trilogy *The Coast of Utopia*. His radio plays include *If You're Glad I'll Be Frank*, *Albert's Bridge*, *Where Are They Now?*, *Artist Descending a Staircase*, *The Dog It Was That Died* and *In the Native State*. Work for television includes *Professional Foul* and *Squaring the Circle*. His film credits include *Empire of the Sun*, *Rosencrantz and Guildenstern Are Dead*, which he also directed, *Shakespeare in Love* (with Marc Norman) and *Enigma*.

TONY HARRISON was born in Leeds in 1937. His volumes of poetry include *The Loiners* (winner of the Geoffrey Faber Memorial Prize), *Continuous*, v. (broadcast on Channel 4 in 1987, winning the Royal Television Society Award), *The Gaze of the Gorgon* (winner of the Whitbread Prize for poetry), *Laureate's Block* and *Under the Clock, New Poems* (2005). Recognised as Britain's leading theatre and film poet, his work includes *The Misanthrope*, *Phaedra Britannica*, *Bow Down*, *The Mysteries*, *The Oresteia* and *The Prince's Play*, all written for the National Theatre, for which he also wrote and directed *The Trackers of Oxyrhynchus* and *Square Rounds*. His most recent work for the theatre was a version of *Hecuba* for the RSC (2005). His many films include *Black Daisies for the Bride* (winner of the Prix Italia in 1994) and, as writer and director, *The Shadow of Hiroshima*, *Prometheus* and his most recent film/poem, *Crossings* (2002). He was the recipient of the Northern Rock Foundation Writer's Award 2004.

CHRISTOPHER HAMPTON was born in the Azores in 1946. He wrote his first play, *When Did You Last See My Mother?*, at the age of eighteen. Since then, his plays have included *The Philanthropist*, *Savages*, *Tales from Hollywood*, *Les Liaisons Dangereuses*, *White Chameleon* and *The Talking Cure*. He has translated plays by Ibsen, Molière, von Horváth, Chekhov and Yasmina Reza (including *Art* and *Life x 3*). His television work includes adaptations of *The History Man* and *Hotel du Lac*. His screenplays include *The Honorary Consul*, *The Good Father*, *Dangerous Liaisons*, *Mary Reilly*, *Total Eclipse*, *The Quiet American*, *Carrington*, *The Secret Agent* and *Imagining Argentina*, the last three of which he also directed.

FRANK MCGUINNESS was born in Buncrana, Co. Donegal, and now lives in Dublin and lectures in English at University College Dublin. His plays include: *The Factory Girls* (Abbey Theatre, Dublin, 1982), *Baglady* (Abbey, 1985), *Observe the Sons of Ulster Marching Towards the Somme* (Abbey, 1985; Hampstead Theatre, London, 1986), *Innocence* (Gate Theatre, Dublin, 1986), *Carthaginians* (Abbey, 1988; Hampstead, 1989), *Mary and Lizzie* (RSC, 1989), *The Bread Man* (Gate, 1991), *Someone Who'll Watch Over Me* (Hampstead, West End and Broadway, 1992), *The Bird Sanctuary* (Abbey, 1994), *Mutabilitie* (NT, 1997), *Dolly West's Kitchen* (Abbey, 1999; Old Vic, 2000), *Gates of Gold* (Gate, 2002) and *Speaking Like Magpies* (RSC, 2005). He has written many translations, including *Rosmersholm*, *Peer Gynt*, *Three Sisters*, *Yerma*, *The Threepenny Opera*, *Hedda Gabler*, *Uncle Vanya*, *A Doll's House*, *The Caucasian Chalk Circle*, *Electra*, *The Storm*, *The Wild Duck* and, most recently, *Hecuba*.